THE TAAS COACH

by
Sheila C. Crowell,
Paula Hartz,
& Ellen D. Kolba

Illustrations by
Michael McDermott

GRADE FIVE
ENGLISH
LANGUAGE ARTS

EDUCATIONAL DESIGN, INC. EDI 050

ACKNOWLEDGEMENTS

The authors wish to thank the following administrators, teachers, and their pupils for their help and participation in the ***TAAS Coach*** pilot project. They were wonderful. Their advice and the sample composition that they contributed have helped shape this book in countless ways.

CORPUS CHRISTI ISD

Cynthia Cardenas
Edna Cleland
Dr. Dawn Dorsey
Judy Maroney
Evie Martin
Chris Pernod-Hough
Melissa Webb

EDINBURG
(Region I Service Center)

Anna Alizen
Hilda Escobar

ARLINGTON ISD

Karen Vosdoganes

HUMBLE ISD

Judy Johnson
Dr. Jane Nelson

DALLAS ISD

Dana Brooks
Sandy Gorman
Marjorie King
Karen Lopez
Terry McPhail
Conchis Silva
Louise Smith

HOUSTON AREA SCHOOLS

Roger Bunnell
Carolyn Lockett
Calvin Raines

ISBN# 0-87694-387-3 EDI 050

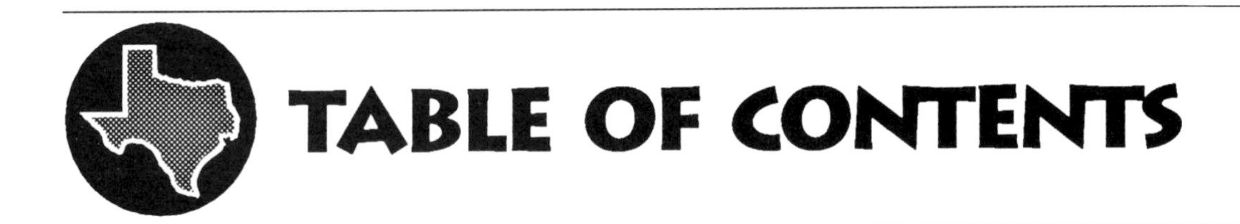

TABLE OF CONTENTS

SECTION A
READING COMPREHENSION

SECTION B – WRITING, PART 1
WRITTEN COMPOSITION

VOLUME 1

UNIT **1**

The Anglo-Saxon and Medieval Periods

Origin of a Nation

UNIT **2**

The English Renaissance

A Celebration of Human Achievement

UNIT **3**

The Restoration and the 18th Century

Tradition and Reason

VOLUME 2

UNIT **4**

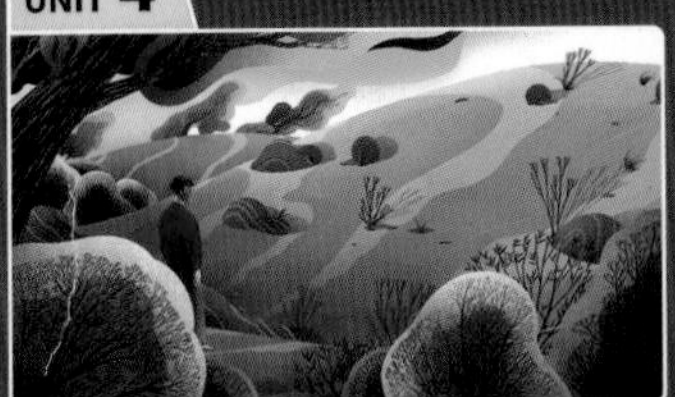

The Flowering of Romanticism

Emotion and Experimentation

UNIT **5**

The Victorians

An Era of Rapid Change

UNIT **6**

Modern and Contemporary Literature

New Ideas, New Voices

GRADE 12 VOL 2

ISBN 978-0-358-41647-0

90000 >

9 780358 416470

1791534

Houghton Mifflin Harcourt.
The Learning Company

SECTION C – WRITING, PART 2
MULTIPLE-CHOICE QUESTIONS

BEFORE YOU BEGIN

WHAT IS THE TAAS TEST?

What is TAAS?

The TAAS tests are special tests that are given in Texas. They test you on English (reading and writing) and math. The name TAAS comes from the full name of the tests—**T**exas **A**ssessment of **A**cademic **S**kills.

Who gets tested, and when?

Every October, Texas gives TAAS tests to students in grades 3, 5, 7, 9, and 11. This book is about only one of these tests—the 5th-grade test for English language arts.

What is the test like?

The Reading test contains reading passages and multiple-choice questions. The questions test how well you understand the reading passages. They also test how clearly you think about what the passages say.

The Writing test has two parts.

In Part 1, you are asked to write a composition on a topic that the test gives you.

In Part 2, you are asked to identify or correct the writing errors in several short passages.

Except for your composition, all the questions are multiple choice. You will see lots of examples in this book.

When will I know how well I did?

Your school will have your scores by the end of October, except for the written composition. You'll get your scores for the written composition in December.

Can I study for TAAS?

Of course. That's what this book is for.

WHAT WILL THE TAAS COACH DO?

The TAAS Coach will do what any good coach does. A coach shows you what you have to do to be a winner.

The TAAS Coach will do the following things for you:

- **A coach checks out your strengths and weaknesses.**

  The TAAS Coach checks you out on practice TAAS tests and shows you exactly what you need to work on.

- **A coach explains the rules and goals of the game.**

  The TAAS Coach explains what the test is. It shows you what kinds of questions will be asked. It tells you what the test-makers are looking for.

- **A coach serves as a model for you to imitate and learn from.**

  The TAAS Coach shows you the thinking process you can follow to get the answer to each question. Special *"Think Along"* sections will give you models to follow.

- **A coach gives you instruction and drills that improve your skills.**

  The TAAS Coach gives you instructions on how to handle every kind of question that may be on the TAAS test. And it contains sample tests for you to practice your skills on.

- **A coach gives you tips that give you a special "edge."**

  The TAAS Coach is filled with these.

- **A coach shows you how to outsmart your opponents.**

  The TAAS Coach does this, too. You'll learn about the traps hidden in the answer choices. And you'll learn how to avoid them.

We call this book *The TAAS Coach* because it contains all the instruction you need to be a winner. But you are still the one who has to take the test. In the end, *The TAAS Coach* is only as good as you are. The more effort you put in, the better you will do on the TAAS test.

Good luck on the TAAS Test!

SECTION A READING COMPREHENSION

A: READING COMPREHENSION SECTION GUIDE TO THE TEACHER

The Reading section of *The TAAS Coach* takes students through all sixteen of the instructional targets that may be tested on the TAAS Reading test. It follows the instructional pattern recommended by leading teaching authorities: modeling, followed by guided practice, and then independent practice. With four complete reading tests, twelve reading passages, 64 questions of reading comprehension, and intensive instruction, this section of *The TAAS Coach* contains everything your students need to prepare for the TAAS Reading test.

The Reading section of *The TAAS Coach* consists of five parts:

1. ***Pretest***
2. ***How to Answer TAAS Questions***
3. ***Practice with Tips***
4. ***Practice on Your Own***
5. ***Post-test***

Each part covers all sixteen TAAS instructional targets that 5th-grade students may encounter on the TAAS Reading test.

The ***Pretest*** is a complete sample TAAS Reading test. It contains 3 reading passages followed by five or six questions each. It is used to acquaint students with the test format and to assess their ability to handle individual targets. Further practice can be individualized based on the results of the pretest.

How to Answer TAAS Questions reviews the questions of the Pretest. This section models the type of thinking that students need to pursue when answering TAAS questions. It examines each question in order, using "Think Along" models to help students develop strategies for answering each type of question. These "Think-Along" sections are the heart of each lesson. You may wish to read them aloud, or to have selected students read them aloud.

This section may be used individually, in small groups, or in whole-class settings. Where time permits, students may go through all the lessons in this section.

For speed, each student can be assigned work on only those lessons that review Pretest questions that he or she missed.

Practice with Tips is a second complete sample test, consisting of three new reading test passages plus questions. This section gives students guided practice in answering TAAS questions. Helpful hints printed in the margin next to each question remind the student of the important strategies learned in the previous section on How to Answer TAAS Questions.

Practice on Your Own is a third complete sample test with questions. This section gives students independent practice on taking the exam. No hints are given on how to answer the questions.

The ***Post-test*** is a final check of students' mastery of the test objectives and format.

A: READING COMPREHENSION SECTION GUIDE TO THE STUDENT

The TAAS Reading exam tests how well you understand what you read. It also tests whether you can think logically about what you read.

To do well on the TAAS Reading test, you do not need to learn any new facts. It does help, however, to know some strategies that will help you be a better test taker.

This section of *The TAAS Coach* will show you how to answer the kinds of questions you will meet on the test.

TIPS ON READING A TAAS READING PASSAGE

1. ***Read each reading passage carefully and thoroughly***. Read it all the way through. Read it twice if you need to. Be sure you understand it.

2. ***Take your time.*** Do not hurry. You will have plenty of time.

3. ***Remember your basic reading skills.*** For example, you should know how to find a main idea, how to put things in time order, and how to use context clues to figure out word meanings.

4. ***Don't read the questions before you read the selection.*** They will just confuse you.

TIPS ON CHOOSING THE RIGHT ANSWER

Remember that only one answer is correct. All the information you need to answer the question is in the passage.

Here are some important tips.

1. ***Read all the choices.*** Even if you are sure you've found the correct answer choice, don't mark your answer sheet until you have looked at every one.

2. ***Write in your booklet.*** You can underline ideas or make notes in the margin. Notes can help you find important ideas again quickly.

3. ***Answer all the questions.*** A good guess is better than nothing.

4. ***Find support for your answer in the passage.*** You must be able to say to yourself, "This answer choice is correct because the passage says . . . "

Sometimes the supporting words will be exactly the same as the answer choice. Other times the supporting words will be different but will mean the same thing. Sometimes the support will be ideas about the passage that make sense. ***But any answer choice that is NOT supported is wrong.***

5. ***Think!*** On this test, you are expected to use your ability to think and reason.

6. ***Eliminate wrong answers.*** If you don't know the right answer, ask yourself why each choice is wrong. The one that's left is probably right.

Sample Passage A

Food from the Desert

If you lived in the desert, do you think you could find or grow your own food? The hot, dry climate of a desert is harsh and inhospitable to gardens. Yet for more than a thousand years, the Pima Indians of Arizona have lived in the desert. They get their food from sturdy plants that grow well there.

Traditional Foods

A Pima woman could make a main-dish stew from native corn, seed pods, and local beans called tepary beans. She picked the leaves and tender parts of green plants for salad and vegetables. She ground the pods of the mesquite plant into flour for bread. Cactus fruit was dessert. In traditional Pima cooking, a whole meal could come from desert plants.

Then something happened to change the Pimas' diet. During World War II, many Pimas left the desert to join the army. When they came home, they brought with them a taste for different foods. The desert foods they had eaten before seemed old fashioned. It was easier to buy something from a store. Soon most of the Pima tribe had stopped eating traditional foods. Instead they ate what everybody else ate.

Why Were the Pimas Sick?

After a time, doctors noticed that many Pimas were becoming sick, but the diseases they had were not caused by germs. Their bodies were just not working properly. But why? Finally the doctors figured out the mystery. The problem was the Pimas' diet. When they ate native foods, their bodies were healthy and strong. When they ate foods like hamburgers, french fries, ice cream, and cookies that they bought at the store, their health suffered. The doctors put one very sick man on a diet of tepary beans, cactus buds, and mesquite pods. Soon, he no longer needed medicine to live. All he needed was a traditional diet.

Science and Desert Foods

Scientists are now studying desert plants. They have found that these plants are rich in vitamins and minerals. Tepary beans, mesquite, and other plants contain protein. One tablespoon of buds from a cholla cactus has as much calcium as a glass of milk. The foods also contain healthful fiber. Many of them taste really good, too.

Now scientists are asking another question. If the traditional diet of Pima Indians is better for the Pimas, would it be better for everyone? Many people might benefit from eating traditional Native American foods. Perhaps someday we will all be saying, "Please pass me the cactus buds," or "Would you like more mesquite?"

Use Prefixes and Suffixes

1 In this passage, the word inhospitable means—

A helpful

B eager

C not friendly

D not in a hospital

Identify Stated or Paraphrased Main Idea

2 What is the main idea of the second paragraph?

A Pima women were good cooks.

B The Pimas could make a complete meal from desert plants.

C Cactus fruit can be eaten for dessert.

D Tepary beans, seed pods, and native corn make a stew.

Predict Probable Future Actions and Outcomes

3 Because of what they have learned from the Pimas, doctors are likely to—

A Give up using medicine.

B Treat people with cactus.

C Try to find out more about desert foods.

D Advise people to eat more hamburger.

Draw Logical Conclusions

4 What did the doctors decide about the change in the Pimas' diet?

A Traditional foods were better for the Pimas.

B Food bought in stores was better for the Pimas.

C It was easier to buy food than to gather it.

D The Pimas' illness was a mystery.

Distinguish Between Fact and Nonfact

5 Which of the following statements about desert foods is an OPINION expressed in the passage?

A Many desert foods contain vitamins.

B Mesquite pods can be ground up for flour.

C Studying desert plants is fun.

D Many desert foods are really delicious.

Sample Passage B

Where Was Kelly's Car Made?

On Monday morning Kelly came to school very excited. "My mother has a new car," she explained. Everybody wanted to know what the car was like. "It's red," Kelly told them.

"Where was your new car made?" asked Ms. Jackson. Kelly did not know. "Today," Ms. Jackson said, "we are starting a new project. We will find out where the things we use are made. We can begin with cars. Where could we go to look at cars?"

Everyone thought that a parking lot would be a good place. So they all went to the town lot to count cars. Kelly was happy that she got to work with Miguel. He already knew many kinds of cars. However, even Miguel did not know where the cars were made.

When their lists were done, Ms. Jackson helped them put all their lists together to compile a single list of all the cars in the parking lot.

Ms. Jackson said, "Some of these cars were made in America. Some were made in Japan, and some were made in Europe. For homework, try to find out where the cars on our list were made. You may ask your parents to help you. Find out as many as you can and bring your list back tomorrow."

The next day the class returned with their lists. Ms. Jackson wrote three words on the chalkboard. They were America, Europe, and Japan. "Now," Ms. Jackson said, "let's see how many cars come from each place."

After the class had added up the numbers of cars, Ms. Jackson asked them, "How can we show this information so it will be easy to see and understand?"

Everybody thought about that. Then Kelly said, "We could make a picture graph! The pictures could be little cars." The class decided that was a good idea. Ms. Jackson showed them how to make a picture graph of their information.

"The first part is done," she explained. "You already know how many cars come from each place. Next you have to decide how many cars to draw. You don't want to draw ninety pictures. Choose the number of cars each car picture will mean."

"I see," said Kelly. "Counting ninety pictures would be almost as hard as counting the ninety cars! Let's make each picture stand for ten cars."

"That's good," said Ms. Jackson. "Then draw the number of cars you need on the graph. Put the biggest number on top. Put the smallest number on the bottom. On the side, label each row with the place where the cars come from. Under your graph, be sure to show how many cars each picture means. Finally, don't forget to give your graph a title."

Kelly, Miguel, and their classmates worked hard on their graph. When they finished it, they put it on the wall. It looked really good. "There were more American cars than Japanese cars or European cars," Miguel said. "I never noticed that before. With the chart, it's easy to see."

"That's why we made the chart," said Kelly. "And now I know that my mother's new car was made in America, too."

AMERICAN AND FOREIGN CARS

Each [car] means 10 cars counted

Use Context Clues

1 The word <u>compile</u> in this passage means—

- **A** park
- **B** bring together
- **C** say how things are alike
- **D** separate

Follow Directions

2 What was the first step in making the graph?

- **A** Writing the title
- **B** Writing labels on the rows
- **C** Picking a color for each car picture
- **D** Counting the cars from each place

Describe the Setting

3 Where does most of this story take place?

- **A** In Kelly's mother's car
- **B** In Ms. Jackson's classroom
- **C** In a car showroom
- **D** In the parking lot

Identify the Best Summary

4 Which statement is the best summary of this story?

- **A** Ms. Jackson shows Kelly's class how to make a picture graph about cars.
- **B** Kelly's mother gets a new car that is made in America and Kelly gets to ride in it.
- **C** Ms. Jackson 's class counts cars in a parking lot.
- **D** A class learns something new.

Interpret Graphic Aids

5 According to the picture graph, which statement about the cars in the parking lot is true?

- **A** There were more European cars than Japanese cars.
- **B** There were forty Japanese cars.
- **C** There were more American cars than Japanese cars.
- **D** There were more Japanese cars than American cars.

Understand Characters' Feelings and Emotions

6 How do Kelly and her classmates feel about the finished graph?

- **A** disappointed
- **B** pleased
- **C** worried
- **D** angry

Sample Passage C

How Does the Lead Get Inside a Pencil?

The next time you pick up a pencil, take a close look. What is it made of? There are two cylinders. The outer one—the one you are holding—is a long, round piece of wood. The inner cylinder is called the lead. This is the part of the pencil that makes black marks on the paper. Without the lead, you would just have a hunk of wood. With the lead, you have a pencil.

In order to make pencils, people needed first to discover how to make a pencil lead. The first step was the discovery of graphite. This form of natural carbon is related to coal. But it was not discovered until 1500. There were two kinds of graphite. One was solid and could be picked up easily. The other was soft and crumbly.

At the start, people wrote with pieces of solid graphite. They wrapped the graphite in sheepskin. However, solid graphite was rare and very expensive. Scientists began looking for an inexpensive way to make a writing tool.

In 1795, a Frenchman found a way to mix clay with the less expensive, crumbly kind of graphite. When the mixture was baked in a special kind of very hot oven, it became solid and easy to write with.

Today, pencil leads are made by adding ground-up graphite to a mixture of clay and water. Then the water is removed, leaving a solid cake. This cake is ground up again to make a fine powder. More water is added. Now the mixture is like dough. The graphite mixture can then be pushed into one end of a hollow tube. When it squeezes out through the other end, it is one very long, soft pencil lead. Finally, the lead is cut into pencil-length pieces and then baked until it is hard.

So how do they slide the lead into the hole in the pencil? They don't. Instead, the wood is in two pieces. Each piece is shaped on the inside to fit around the pencil lead. The pieces of wood are glued into place around the lead. Then they are painted. Look at your own pencil again. Now can you see how it is made?

Understand Specialized/Technical Terms

1 The word graphite in this passage means—

A a pencil
B a way of discovering things
C a form of carbon
D a piece of wood

Identify Implied Main Idea

2 What is the fifth paragraph mostly about?

A How graphite is ground up
B How pencil leads are made
C How graphite was discovered
D How pencils are put together

Arrange Events in Sequential Order

3 What do pencil-makers do right after they push the graphite mixture through a hollow tube?

A Mix it with water
B Glue it onto wood
C Polish it
D Cut it into pencil lengths

Identify Cause and Effect

4 Why do pencil-makers use crumbly graphite instead of solid graphite?

A Solid graphite is too hard to write with.
B Crumbly graphite is easier to work with.
C Crumbly graphite doesn't cost as much.
D Crumbly graphite can be baked.

Recall Supporting Facts and Details

5 How did the Frenchman make crumbly graphite solid enough to use in pencils?

A By grinding it up and glueing it together
B By wrapping it in sheepskin and tying it
C By mixing it with lead and melting it
D By mixing it with clay and baking it

LESSON A1 PREFIXES & SUFFIXES

TARGET: Use prefixes and suffixes to determine word meanings.

SAMPLE PASSAGE A "FOOD FROM THE DESERT"

Here's how to answer a question like Question 1 that follows Sample Reading Passage A, "Food from the Desert."

Turn to the reading passage.

QUESTION 1

1 In this passage, the word inhospitable means—

A helpful

B eager

C not friendly

D not in a hospital

STEPS TO THE ANSWER

1. Turn back to the reading passage. Read the sentence with the underlined word in it. Read the sentence before it and after it. Somewhere in these sentences is a clue to the word's meaning. Try to guess what it is.

2. Take each answer choice. Put it in place of the underlined word. Read the new sentence with the answer choice word in it. Does it make good sense? Only one answer choice does. This is the correct answer.

3. See if the word has any prefixes or suffixes that you know. Prefixes often give you a clue to a word's meaning. For example, you know that the prefix *un-* means "not" or "opposite." You can guess that "not ready" is a good answer choice for a word like *un*prepared.

THINK-ALONG

This is the way you should think when you answer the question.

Read this part slowly and carefully. Your teacher may also read it aloud to you. Look at the answer choices and the passage when you need to.

Before I do anything else, let me see what I can figure out about this word. The prefix is *in-*. I think *in-* means "not" or "the opposite of"—at least it does in words like inactive and incomplete. The suffix *-able* can mean "able to," but "able to hospit" doesn't help me much. Well, anyway, I'm looking for a meaning with not in it. Now I'll look at the answers.

- A is "helpful." Let me read it in the sentence—"The hot, dry climate of a desert is harsh and helpful to gardens." That's all wrong. The climate is hot, dry, and harsh. It isn't helpful to gardens at all.
- B is "eager." Let me read it in the sentence—"The hot, dry climate of a desert is harsh and eager to gardens." This one doesn't make any sense at all. So this is wrong.
- C is "not friendly." Hey, that sounds right! "The hot, dry climate of a desert is harsh and not friendly to gardens." I like this one. And it has the meaning "not" in it. But I know I have to look at all the answers, so I'll look at the last one.
- D is "not in a hospital." Another answer with the meaning "not" in it. And inhospitable sounds a little like hospital—but wait. Let me put it into the sentence. "The hot, dry climate of a desert is harsh and not in a hospital to gardens." That makes no sense at all! This one is wrong.

I'm choosing C.

DON'T BE FOOLED BY TRAPS

a. A word that means the opposite of the underlined word (like Choice A)

b. A word with a similar spelling to the underlined word (like Choice D)

c. A word that is just plain wrong (like Choice B)

REMEMBER

Put each answer choice into the passage in place of the underlined word. Pick the one that makes sense there.

LESSON A2 THE MAIN IDEA

TARGET: Identify the stated or paraphrased main idea of a selection.

SAMPLE PASSAGE A "FOOD FROM THE DESERT"

Here's how to answer a question like Question 2 that follows the Sample Reading Passage "Food from the Desert."

Turn to the reading passage.

QUESTION 2

2 What is the main idea of the second paragraph?

A Pima women were good cooks.

B The Pimas could make a complete meal from desert plants.

C Cactus fruit is good to eat.

D Tepary beans, seed pods, and native corn make a stew.

STEPS TO THE ANSWER

1. Remember what a main idea is. It is the most important idea in the passage. The other ideas are details.
2. Turn back to the passage and read the part the question asks for. Look for the main idea. All of the answers may be true statements from the passage, but only one is the main idea.
3. If you're looking for the main idea of a paragraph, look at the first sentence and the last sentence. One of these sentences often tells you what the paragraph is mainly about. A sentence like this is called the topic sentence.
4. If you're looking for the main idea of a whole selection, look at the first paragraph and the last paragraph. They often state the main idea.

THINK-ALONG

This is the way you should think when you answer the question.

Read this part slowly and carefully. Your teacher may also read it aloud to you. Look at the answer choices and the passage when you need to.

- A is "Pima women were good cooks." Maybe they were, but the second paragraph doesn't say that. I'm looking for a stated main idea—one that's already in there. I don't see this anywhere, so I'm going on.
- B is "The Pimas could make a complete meal from desert plants." This is true. The passage says so. The passage is full of details about this. And here, in the last sentence, it says "the whole meal came from desert plants." Close enough. I think this is the right answer, but I'm going to check out the others anyway.
- C is "Cactus fruit can be eaten for dessert." This is in the passage, but it's a detail, not a main idea. The main idea is about the whole meal, and dessert is just a part of it. This is not the answer.
- D is "Tepary beans, seed pods, and native corn make a stew." This is about what the first sentence says, but it's not the main idea. It's another detail. This answer is wrong.

The right answer is B.

DON'T BE FOOLED BY TRAPS

a. An answer that is a detail, not a main idea (like Choices C and D)

b. An answer that might be true, but is not in the passage (like Choice A)

REMEMBER

Be sure the answer you choose is the main idea, not just an important detail.

LESSON A3 PREDICTING ACTIONS & OUTCOMES

TARGET: Predict probable future actions and outcomes.

SAMPLE PASSAGE A "FOOD FROM THE DESERT"

Here's how to answer a question like Question 3 that follows the Sample Reading Passage "Food from the Desert."

Turn to the reading passage.

QUESTION 3

3 Because of what they have learned from the Pimas, doctors are likely to—

A give up using medicine

B treat people with cactus

C try to find out more about desert foods

D advise people to eat more hamburger

STEPS TO THE ANSWER

1. Try to answer the question yourself. How would you complete the sentence? Then look at each answer choice in turn. Try to find the answer you came up with, or a better one.

2. Pick the answer that makes the most sense. The best answer will be logical. It will be supported by the facts in the story. It will not be a trick answer or a surprise.

THINK-ALONG

This is the way you should think when you answer the question.

Read this part slowly and carefully. Your teacher may also read it aloud to you. Look at the answer choices and the passage when you need to.

- A is "give up using medicine." Well, I don't think doctors are likely to do that any time soon. That isn't logical. Nothing in the reading passage supports it. This is a No.
- B is "treat people with cactus." Doctors might advise people to eat desert foods, but that's not the same as treating them with cactus. Even if cactus was good for one sickness, it might not be good for another. This isn't supported by the story. Another wrong answer.
- C is "try to find out more about desert foods." This makes sense. The story says, "Scientists are now studying desert plants." They probably don't know everything yet, so they want to know more. I think this is the right answer. But I'll check the last one anyway.
- D is "Advise people to eat more hamburger." No. The passage says that the hamburger and stuff the Pimas were eating made them sick. Doctors wouldn't advise people to do more of something that was making them sick. No way.

C is the best answer here.

DON'T BE FOOLED BY TRAPS

a. Surprise answers that don't belong with the story (like A)

b. Answers that are the opposite of logical ones (like D)

c. Answers that aren't supported by the story (like B)

REMEMBER

When you are asked to make a guess about what will happen next, look for an answer that seems logical and makes sense with the rest of the passage.

LESSON A4
DRAWING CONCLUSIONS

TARGET: Draw logical conclusions.

SAMPLE PASSAGE A
"FOOD FROM THE DESERT"

Here's how to answer a question like Question 4 that follows the Sample Reading Passage "Food from the Desert."

Turn to the reading passage.

QUESTION 4

4 Why did the doctors want to change the Pimas' diet?

A Traditional foods were better for the Pimas.

B Food bought in stores was better for the Pimas.

C It was easier to buy food than to gather it.

D The Pimas' illness was a mystery.

STEPS TO THE ANSWER

Skim the reading passage to find the part about the doctors and the Pimas' illnesses. The heading "Why Were the Pimas Sick?" will help you find it. Try to find the answer to the question there.

The correct answer must be based on what the passage says. It must be supported by facts in the passage.

THINK-ALONG

This is the way you should think when you answer the question.

Read this part slowly and carefully. Your teacher may also read it aloud to you. Look at the answer choices and the passage when you need to.

- A is "Traditional foods were better for the Pimas." The passage doesn't say this, exactly, but it says the Pimas were healthy when they ate native foods. So the native foods were probably better for them. I think this could be the right answer. But I know I have to check the others anyway.
- B is "Food bought in stores was better for the Pimas." I don't think so. The passage says when they ate food from the stores, they got sick. So the food couldn't be better for them. This answer is wrong.
- C is "It was easier to buy food than to gather it." That's probably true, but it doesn't answer the question. It doesn't tell why the doctors wanted to change the Pimas' diet. This is wrong, too.
- D is "The Pima's illness was a mystery." But the passage says, "the doctors figured out the mystery." So it wasn't a mystery any more. This is another wrong answer.

The right answer is A.

DON'T BE FOOLED BY TRAPS

a. Answers that are the opposite of what the story says (like B and D)

b. Answers that might be true, but that aren't supported by the story or that don't answer the question (like C)

REMEMBER

When you draw a conclusion, look for ideas and information in the reading passage that will support your choice.

LESSON A5
FACT & NONFACT

TARGET: Distinguish between fact and nonfact.

SAMPLE PASSAGE A
"FOOD FROM THE DESERT"

Here's how to answer a question like Question 5 that follows the Sample Reading Passage "Food from the Desert."

Turn to the reading passage.

QUESTION 5

5 Which of the following statements about desert foods is an OPINION?

A Many desert foods contain vitamins.

B Mesquite pods can be ground up for flour.

C Studying desert plants is fun.

D Many desert foods are delicious.

STEPS TO THE ANSWER

1. Know the difference between facts and opinions.
   - A *fact* is something you can prove. You can look it up. Or you can observe it. Or you can do both.
   - An *opinion* expresses someone's feelings, ideas, or beliefs. An opinion cannot be proved. People can have different opinions.
2. Look for opinion words. They signal that a statement is an opinion. Here are some important ones.
   - Words like *good, bad, best, worst, least, most*, etc.
   - Words like *pretty, ugly, boring, yummy, nicer*, etc.
   - Words like *hate, love, like, dislike,* etc.
   - Words like *believe, hope, feel, think,* etc.
   - Words like *should, should not, ought to,* etc.
3. Decide whether each answer choice is what the question asks for—a fact or an opinion. If it is, then try to find it in the passage. If an answer choice is not in the passage, it's wrong.

THINK-ALONG

This is the way you should think when you answer the question.

Read this part slowly and carefully. Your teacher may also read it aloud to you. Look at the answer choices and the passage when you need to.

I have to find an OPINION that is in the passage. All right—that's something that cannot be looked up or proved. Here goes.

- A is "Many desert foods contain vitamins." That's a fact. It's something scientists have found out. I want an opinion. This is not the correct answer choice.
- B is "Mesquite pods can be ground up for flour." That's mentioned in paragraph 2. I could observe that, I guess. So it's another fact. I want an opinion.
- C is "Studying desert plants is fun." That's an opinion. Some people might think it was fun and some might not. But is it in the passage? No. So it's not the right answer.
- D is "Many desert foods are delicious." Delicious is an opinion word—what I think is delicious, somebody else might think was yuckky. And it's in the passage—here in paragraph 5.

I guess D is the right answer.

DON'T BE FOOLED BY TRAPS

a. A fact when the question asks for an OPINION (like A and B). Or an opinion when the question asks for a FACT.

b. A fact or opinion that is not in the passage (like C).

REMEMBER

Facts can be looked up or proved, but opinions can't be. Look for opinion words to help you identify opinions.

LESSON A6 CONTEXT CLUES

TARGET: Use context clues to determine the meaning of an unfamiliar word.

SAMPLE PASSAGE B

"WHERE WAS KELLY'S CAR MADE?"

Here's how to answer a question like Question 1 that follows the Sample Reading Passage "Where Was Kelly's Car Made?"

Turn to the reading passage.

QUESTION 1

1 The word compile in this passage means—

A park

B bring together

C say how things are alike

D separate

STEPS TO THE ANSWER

1. Turn back to the reading passage and find the sentence with the underlined word. Reread the part of the passage where the word appears. The clues may be in the same sentence as the word or in a sentence before it or after it. Think about the answer choices as you read.
2. Take each answer choice and put it in place of the underlined word. Read the new sentence with the answer choice word in it. Does it make good sense? Only one answer choice does. This is the correct answer.

THINK-ALONG

This is the way you should think when you answer the question.

Read this part slowly and carefully. Your teacher may also read it aloud to you. Look at the answer choices and the passage when you need to.

- A is "park" That answer doesn't make sense when you put it in the sentence. You can't park a list. I guess that answer was put in to trap someone who was thinking about parking lots. I'm going to look at another answer.
- B is "bring together." That's just about what the passage says they did—they put their lists together. I like this answer. But I'd better look at them all just to make sure.
- C is "say how things are alike." That's comparing. The words compare and compile sound a little bit alike, but that meaning doesn't make sense in the sentence. You can't compare a single list. You have to compare it with something. This is wrong.
- D is "separate." There is nothing in the passage about separating the lists. The students put their lists together. They didn't separate them. I'm sticking with B. It makes the most sense.

DON'T BE FOOLED BY TRAPS

a. A word that means the opposite of the underlined word (like Choice D)

b. A word with a spelling similar to the underlined word (like Choice C)

c. A word that is just plain wrong (like Choice A)

REMEMBER

Put each answer choice into the passage in place of the underlined word. Pick the one that makes sense there.

LESSON A7
FOLLOWING DIRECTIONS

TARGET: Follow complex directions.

SAMPLE PASSAGE B
"WHERE WAS KELLY'S CAR MADE?"

Here's how to answer a question like Question 2 that follows the Sample Reading Passage "Where Was Kelly's Car Made?"

Turn to the reading passage.

QUESTION 2

2 What was the first step in making the graph?

A Writing the title

B Writing labels on the rows

C Picking a color for each car picture

D Counting the cars from each place

STEPS TO THE ANSWER

1. Reread the part of the passage that gives the directions. Be sure not to skip a single step. Pay special attention to the order in which the steps are given.
2. Now look at the answer choices again. Read them one at a time and think about each one as you read.

THINK-ALONG

This is the way you should think when you answer the question.

Read this part slowly and carefully. Your teacher may also read it aloud to you. Look at the answer choices and the passage when you need to.

- A is "writing the title." I guess they could have done this first. But Ms. Jackson said, "Finally, give your graph a title." So the directions say to do this last. This answer is definitely wrong.
- B is "writing labels on the rows." Ms. Jackson said to do this after they drew the cars. So it's not the first step. This answer is wrong, too.
- C is "picking a color for each car picture." Is this right? I don't find anything about picking colors in the passage. This is definitely wrong.
- D is "count the cars from each place." This looks like the answer. For one thing, it makes sense. It's also what Ms. Jackson said—"The first part is done . . . you know how many cars come from each place." Yes, this is definitely right.

The answer is D.

DON'T BE FOOLED BY TRAPS

a. Answer choices that are out of order (like A and B)

b. Answer choices that list things that are not in the directions (like C)

REMEMBER

Compare the answer choices with the directions in the passage.

LESSON A8
STORY SETTING

***TARGET:* Describe the setting of a story (time and place).**

SAMPLE PASSAGE B
"WHERE WAS KELLY'S CAR MADE?"

Here's how to answer a question like Question 3 that follows the Sample Reading Passage "Where Was Kelly's Car Made?"

Turn to the reading passage.

QUESTION 3

3 Where does most of this story take place?

A In Kelly's mother's car

B In Ms. Jackson's classroom

C In a car showroom

D In the parking lot

STEPS TO THE ANSWER

1. If you have read the story carefully, you may remember the setting. If you do not remember, reread the passage until you think you know the answer.

2. Look for the setting near the beginning of the story. If you do not find it, you may have to put clues together to figure it out.

THINK-ALONG

This is the way you should think when you answer the question.

Read this part slowly and carefully. Your teacher may also read it aloud to you. Look at the answer choices and the passage when you need to.

- A is "in Kelly's mother's car." The beginning of the story is about Kelly's mother's car, but the story doesn't take place there. The car could only be the setting if the story took place inside it or near it. But it doesn't. So this answer is wrong.
- B is "in Ms. Jackson's classroom." Well, the passage says "school" and Ms. Jackson is definitely the teacher. And she writes on the chalkboard. So she must be in a classroom. This answer looks good. But I'll check the rest anyhow.
- C is "in a car showroom." The passage doesn't mention a car showroom at all. This must be put in for people who don't read the passage at all, but just guess. I can rule this answer out, too.
- D is "in the parking lot." They did go to the parking lot. But most of the time they were in Ms. Jackson's room. This isn't right. I'm sure now. I'm sticking with B.

DON'T BE FOOLED BY TRAPS

a. A setting (time or place) that is mentioned in the story, but is not the main setting (like A and D)

b. A setting that is not part of the story at all (like C)

REMEMBER

The setting is often stated near the beginning, or you can use clues in the passage to help you figure it out.

LESSON A9 SUMMARY

TARGET: Identify the best summary of a selection.

SAMPLE PASSAGE B

"WHERE WAS KELLY'S CAR MADE?"

Here's how to answer a question like Question 4 that follows the Sample Reading Passage "Where Was Kelly's Car Made?"

Turn to the reading passage.

QUESTION 4

4 Which statement is the best summary of this story?

A Ms. Jackson shows Kelly's class how to make a picture graph about cars.

B Kelly's mother gets a new car that is made in America, and Kelly gets to ride in it.

C Ms. Jackson's class counts cars in a parking lot.

D A class learns something new.

STEPS TO THE ANSWER

1. Decide what are the most important facts and details of the passage. Who are the most important characters? What are the most important things they do? What is the passage mainly about? Does one of the answers seem to include all the things you chose?
2. Look for an answer that covers the whole passage—not just a part of it.

THINK-ALONG

This is the way you should think when you answer the question.

Read this part slowly and carefully. Your teacher may also read it aloud to you. Look at the answer choices and the passage when you need to.

Before I look at the answers, I'll think about this myself. The story is about Kelly's class and how Ms. Jackson teaches them to make a graph about where cars are made. Now I'll see if I can find a summary like that.

- A is "Ms. Jackson shows Kelly's class how to make a picture graph about cars." That's pretty close to what I thought by myself. It has all the main points I came up with—Ms. Jackson, Kelly, making picture graphs, and cars. This could be the right answer. But I'll see what the other choices say.
- B is "Kelly's mother gets a new car that is made in America, and Kelly gets to ride in it." Well, that's true. But Kelly's mother isn't an important character in the story—she's only mentioned once. The passage doesn't say that Kelly got to ride in the car. Ms. Jackson and the picture graph are not even mentioned. So this answer is wrong.
- C is "Ms Jackson's class counts cars in a parking lot." That's true. But that's only part of what the passage is about. It's only a detail. It doesn't mention the graph at all. This answer is wrong, too.
- D is "A class learns something new." This is true, but it could be about anything. It doesn't include any real facts or details from this passage. It doesn't mention Ms. Jackson or Kelly or cars or graphs. This is another wrong answer.

A is the right answer. It gives the most important facts.

DON'T BE FOOLED BY TRAPS

a. An answer that contains information not in the story (like B)

b. An answer that is a detail, not a summary of the whole passage (like both B and C)

c. An answer that is too broad or too general (like D)

REMEMBER

Choose a summary that covers the whole passage and gives all the important facts.

LESSON A10 GRAPHIC SOURCES

TARGET: Use graphic sources for information.

SAMPLE PASSAGE B

"WHERE WAS KELLY'S CAR MADE?"

Here's how to answer a question like Question 5 that follows the Sample Reading Passage "Where Was Kelly's Car Made?"

Turn to the reading passage.

QUESTION 5

5 According to the picture graph, which statement about the cars in the lot is true?

A There were more European cars than Japanese cars.

B There were forty Japanese cars.

C There were more American cars than Japanese cars.

D There were more Japanese cars than American cars.

STEPS TO THE ANSWER

1. First think about what the question asks you to do. It asks you to find the true statement. You will have to compare the answers with the information on the graph to find the one that is true.

2. The headings on the graphic source are important. Use them to help you find the answer.

THINK-ALONG

This is the way you should think when you answer the question.

Read this part slowly and carefully. Your teacher may also read it aloud to you. Look at the answer choices, the passage, and the graphic source when you need to.

- A is "There were more European cars than Japanese cars." All I have to do is find the European cars and the Japanese cars on the graph and compare them. The row of European cars is shorter than the row of Japanese cars. That means there were not as many European cars. So this answer is definitely wrong.

- B is "There were forty Japanese cars." Well, for this answer I have to know how many cars each car on the graph means, and figure out the number of Japanese cars.

  At the bottom of the graph it says each car means ten cars. Ten, twenty, thirty . . . Not forty. This answer is wrong, too.

- C is "There were more American cars than Japanese cars." This looks right. American cars have the longest line on the graph, and that means the most cars. I like this answer, but I'd better read the last one to make sure.

- D is "There were more Japanese cars than American cars." No. I already know that most cars were American. This is just the opposite of the right answer. It's definitely wrong. I'm marking C as my answer.

DON'T BE FOOLED BY TRAPS

a. Answers that come from reading a graph or chart wrong (like answers A, B, and D)

REMEMBER

Check the graph or chart carefully when you choose your answer. Don't just look at the answer choices.

LESSON A11 UNDERSTANDING FEELINGS & EMOTIONS

TARGET: Understand the feelings and emotions of characters.

SAMPLE PASSAGE B

"WHERE WAS KELLY'S CAR MADE?"

Here's how to answer a question like Question 6 that follows the Sample Reading Passage "Where Was Kelly's Car Made?"

Turn to the reading passage.

QUESTION 6

6 How do Kelly and her classmates feel about the finished graph?

A disappointed

B pleased

C worried

D angry

STEPS TO THE ANSWER

1. Look through the passage for clues about how the characters might feel. Try to come up with an answer on your own. Then look for an answer that is like yours.
2. Check each answer against the information in the passage. See if it makes sense.

THINK-ALONG

This is the way you should think when you answer the question.

Read this part slowly and carefully. Your teacher may also read it aloud to you. Look at the answer choices and the passage when you need to.

- A is "disappointed." I don't see how this could be right. The passage says they worked hard on the graph and when it was done it looked really good. I think they'd be proud of it, not disappointed. This must be wrong.
- B is "pleased." This might be right. They thought it looked good, and when something you've done looks good, you're usually pleased with it. It's something like "proud." I like this answer, but I think I'll read the next two.
- C is "worried." There wasn't anything for them to be worried about. When Kelly and Miguel are talking, they don't sound worried. They sound pretty happy to me. I think this is another wrong answer.
- D is "sad." Well, maybe if you finished something you were really enjoying, you might feel sad. But I don't see any clues that they were sad. The passage says the graph looked good. I think that means they were pleased with it, and I'm sticking with B.

DON'T BE FOOLED BY TRAPS

a. Answers that describe feelings or emotions that are not reasonable for the story. Your answer must be supported by what the reading passage says.

REMEMBER

Look for clues in the passage. Check all answers before you choose one.

LESSON A12 TECHNICAL TERMS

TARGET: Use context clues to determine the meanings of specialized/technical terms.

SAMPLE PASSAGE C "HOW DOES THE LEAD GET INSIDE A PENCIL?"

Here's how to answer a question like Question 1 that follows the Sample Reading Passage "How Does the Lead Get Inside a Pencil?"

Turn to the reading passage.

QUESTION 1

1 The word graphite in this passage means—

A a pencil

B a chart

C a form of carbon

D a piece of wood

STEPS TO THE ANSWER

1. Look at the passage and find the sentence with the underlined word in it. Then reread the part of the passage where the word appears. Read the whole paragraph. The clues may be in the same sentence as the word. Or it may be in sentences before it or after it. Think about the answer choices as you read.
2. Take each answer choice and put it in place of the underlined word. Read the new sentence with the answer choice word in it. Does it make good sense? Only one answer choice does. This is the correct answer.

THINK-ALONG

This is the way you should think when you answer the question.

Read this part slowly and carefully. Your teacher may also read it aloud to you. Look at the answer choices and the passage when you need to.

- A is "a pencil." The passage says that the discovery of graphite was the first step in making pencil lead. The first step in making a pencil couldn't be the discovery of a pencil. That's backwards. You couldn't discover it until it was made! I don't think this is the answer.

- B is "a chart." That's silly. You can't make a pencil lead from a chart. I'll bet this answer is just put in to catch people who notice that the word graphite looks like the word graph and who don't read any further.

- C is "a form of carbon." I'm not sure exactly what carbon is, but that's what the passage says. It calls graphite "This form of natural carbon." That's a pretty big clue. I think this is right, but I'm going to check the last answer.

- D is "a piece of wood." Could the discovery of wood be the first step in learning to make a pencil lead? That's not a very good answer. Pieces of wood must have been around for a long time before people started putting lead inside them. And a piece of wood isn't a pencil without the lead. So this can't be right either.

C is the best answer. I'm going for C.

DON'T BE FOOLED BY TRAPS

a. A word with a similar spelling to the underlined word (like B)

b. A word that is just plain wrong (like A and D)

REMEMBER

Put each answer choice into the passage in place of the underlined word. Pick the one that makes sense there.

LESSON A13
IMPLIED MAIN IDEA

TARGET: Identify the implied main idea of a selections.

SAMPLE PASSAGE C
"HOW DOES THE LEAD GET INSIDE A PENCIL?"

Here's how to answer a question like Question 2 that follows the Sample Reading Passage "How Does the Lead Get Inside a Pencil?"

Turn to the reading passage.

QUESTION 2

2 What is the fifth paragraph mostly about?

A How graphite is ground up

B How pencil leads are made

C How graphite was discovered

D How pencils are put together

STEPS TO THE ANSWER

1. Be sure you understand what the passage is about. If you do not understand it, read it again. The "main idea" is the most important idea in the passage, or what the passage is mainly about. Try to decide for yourself what the main idea is.

2. Read the answer choices. Pick out the one that does the best job of telling what the passage is about. Here's how you might be thinking as you read.

THINK-ALONG

This is the way you should think when you answer the question.

Read this part slowly and carefully. Your teacher may also read it aloud to you. Look at the answer choices and the passage when you need to.

Before I pick an answer, I'll try to figure out the main idea for myself. The passage says pencil leads are made by adding graphite to clay and water. Then other things are done to the graphite to make pencil leads. That seems to be what the passage is about—making pencil leads.

- A is "how graphite is ground up." Well, the passage says ground-up graphite is used, but it doesn't say how the graphite gets that way. Anyway, that's just a detail. I don't think this is right.
- B is "how pencil leads are made." That's close to what I said—making pencil leads. I like this answer. But I'd better check the rest, just in case.
- C is "how graphite was discovered." There's nothing in this paragraph about how graphite was discovered. This is an easy No.
- D is "how pencils are put together." Later on, in paragraph six, it says how pencils are put together. But I'm supposed to be finding the main idea of paragraph five. So this is also wrong.

I'm marking B. It's the best answer.

DON'T BE FOOLED BY TRAPS

a. An answer that is a detail not a main idea (like A)

b. An answer that is not in the paragraph at all (like C)

c. An answer that refers to a different paragraph (like D)

REMEMBER

Be sure the answer you choose is the main idea, not just an important detail.

LESSON A14 SEQUENCE

TARGET: Arrange events in sequential order.

SAMPLE PASSAGE C
"HOW DOES THE LEAD GET INSIDE A PENCIL?"

Here's how to answer a question like Question 3 that follows the Reading Passage "How Does the Lead Get Inside a Pencil?"

Turn to the reading passage.

QUESTION 3

3 What do pencil-makers do right after they push the graphite mixture through a hollow tube?

A Mix it with water

B Glue it onto wood

C Polish it

D Cut it into pencil lengths and bake it

STEPS TO THE ANSWER

1. Be sure you understand what the question is asking. You may be asked to tell what comes first or last, or what comes before or after a particular event.

2. Go back to the passage. This question asks you to find the next step after the graphite goes through the cylinder. You need to find that step and see what comes next.

3. Do not look for the exact words of the answers in the passage. Look for words and phrases that mean the same thing.

THINK-ALONG

This is the way you should think when you answer the question.

Read this part slowly and carefully. Your teacher may also read it aloud to you. Look at the answer choices and the passage when you need to.

First I'll check the passage and find where it talks about the graphite going through the cylinder. Here it is, in the next to the last paragraph. It's near the end.

Now, what comes next? It says,"Finally, the lead is cut into pencil-length pieces and then baked until it is hard." I'll look for an answer that says that.

- A is "mix it with water." This is one of the things that pencil-makers do, but they do it before they push the graphite through the tube, not after. So this can't be the right answer.
- B is "glue it onto wood." Well, the last paragraph says, "The pieces of wood are glued into place around the lead." That's after the graphite goes through the cylinder. But it's not the next step after. It's not the answer I'm looking for.
- C is "polish it." The passage doesn't say anything about polishing a pencil lead. This is another wrong answer, put in to trap people who don't read the passage carefully.
- D is "cut it into pencil lengths and bake it." This is the answer I've been looking for. D is right.

DON'T BE FOOLED BY TRAPS

a. An answer that is not in the order that the question asks for (like A and B)

b. An answer that is not in the passage at all (like C)

c. The event mentioned first in the passage may not have happened first. The writer may have put it first because it's important, not because it happened first. Don't let this trap catch you if the question asks "what happened first."

REMEMBER

1. Be sure you know what the question is asking you to find. Look for clue words in the passage like first, last, before, and after.
2. Try to find the answer in the passage before you look at the answer choices.

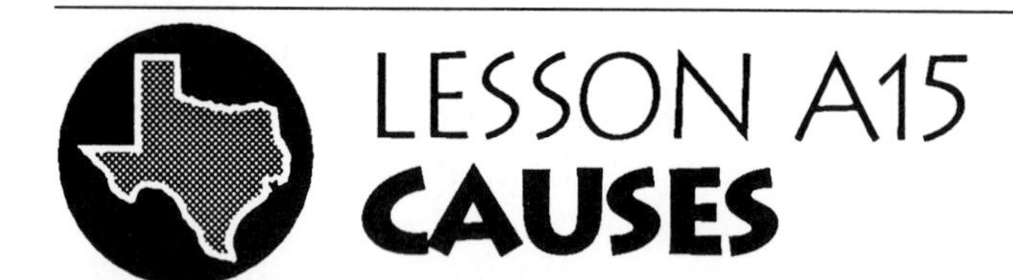

LESSON A15
CAUSES

TARGET: Identify the causes of a given event or a character's actions.

SAMPLE PASSAGE C
"HOW DOES THE LEAD GET INSIDE A PENCIL?"

Here's how to answer a question like Question 4 that follows the Sample Reading Passage "How Does the Lead Get Inside a Pencil?"

Turn to the reading passage.

QUESTION 4

4 Why did pencil-makers use crumbly graphite instead of solid graphite?

A Solid graphite was too hard to write with.

B Crumbly graphite was easier to work with.

C Solid graphite was too expensive.

D Crumbly graphite could be baked.

STEPS TO THE ANSWER

1. Pay attention to what the question is asking. Often the question or the answer will contain clue words like because, since, or as a result. The answer to this "Why" question will be the cause of the pencil-makers' actions.

2. Look over the passage and try to answer the question yourself, before you look at the answers. Then compare your answer with the answers on the test. The closest one is probably right.

THINK-ALONG

This is the way you should think when you answer the question.

Read this part slowly and carefully. Your teacher may also read it aloud to you. Look at the answer choices and the passage when you need to.

First, I need to think about what this question is asking. Another way to ask this question is "Pencil-makers used crumbly graphite because—." It says here that solid graphite was rare and very expensive. That's a reason—they couldn't get it or it cost too much. I'll look for an answer like that.

- A is "Solid graphite was too hard to write with." This can't be the answer. The passage says they did write with it. It was just too expensive. I'll go on.
- B is "Crumbly graphite was easier to work with." I don't think something crumbly would be easier to work with than something solid. This doesn't make good sense. I'll go on.
- C is "Solid graphite cost too much." This is the same as being expensive, the answer I thought of. I like this, but I know I'd better check the last answer anyway to be sure.
- D is "Crumbly graphite could be baked." This is true, but that's not the reason they used it. They baked it to make it solid, not because the crumbly stuff was better. Solid graphite was too expensive, that's all.

I'm sticking with C.

DON'T BE FOOLED BY TRAPS

a. Answers that are the opposite of what the passage says (like A)

b. Answers that don't make sense (like B)

c. Answers that give correct information, but that don't answer the question (like D)

REMEMBER

Read the passage and try to answer the question in your own words before you look at the answers. Then pick the one closest to your own.

LESSON A16
SUPPORTING DETAILS

TARGET: Recall supporting facts and details.

SAMPLE PASSAGE C
"HOW DOES THE LEAD GET INSIDE A PENCIL?"

Here's how to answer a question like Question 5 that follows the Sample Reading Passage "How Does the Lead Get Inside a Pencil?"

Turn to the reading passage.

QUESTION 5

5 How did the Frenchman make crumbly graphite solid enough to use in pencils?

A By grinding it up

B By wrapping it in sheepskin

C By mixing it with lead

D By baking it in a special oven

STEPS TO THE ANSWER

1. Read the passage and find the answer. It's a detail, and will probably be easy to find. Remember, however, that the correct answer choice may have exactly the same words as the passage. But the meaning will be the same.

2. You may think that you remember the detail that the question asks for from your first reading of the passage. But you should still go back to the passage. Find the place that talks about this detail. Reread it to make sure your answer is right.

THINK-ALONG

This is the way you should think when you answer the question.

Read this part slowly and carefully. Your teacher may also read it aloud to you. Look at the answer choices and the passage when you need to.

- A is "by grinding it up." You don't make something solid by grinding it up. This answer is wrong.
- B is "by wrapping it in sheepskin." The passage says they did this with solid graphite, not crumbly graphite. Another No.
- C is "by mixing it with lead and melting it." We call the graphite in a pencil "lead," but the passage doesn't say there's any lead mixed in with the graphite. And melting it wouldn't make it solid. No to this answer, too.
- D is "by baking it in a special oven." Paragraph 4 says that when the mixture was baked in a special kind of hot oven, it became solid. That was the Frenchman's important discovery. This is the right answer.

I'm choosing D.

DON'T BE FOOLED BY TRAPS

a. Answers that don't make sense (like A)

b. Answers that contain a detail from the passage, but not the detail you are looking for (like B)

c. Answers that are based on statements that are not in the passage (like C)

REMEMBER

If the question asks for a detail, be sure you can find that detail in the passage.

SECTION A PRACTICE WITH TIPS

Sample Passage D

How Did America Get Its Name?

Leif Ericsson of Iceland was probably the first explorer from Europe to reach America. However, he does not get much credit for its discovery. The credit usually goes to Christopher Columbus, who was the first European explorer to reach America after Europeans began keeping track of history. The land these two explorers found, however, is not called Ericssonia or Columbia, but America. Where did the name America come from?

Columbus's Discovery

By the time of Columbus, Europeans had forgotten Leif Ericsson's discovery. But sailors were always looking for better ways to get where they wanted to go. Columbus wanted to go to Asia. He thought he could do this by sailing west from Europe, around the world to Asia.

However, Columbus did not know how big the world really is. In his time, European ideas about geography were imprecise. Some people said the world was about 25,000 miles around. Some said it was only 12,000 miles around. Columbus had no way of knowing that a large body of land lay between Europe and Asia. So when he reached land, he thought it was Asia. He never knew that he had found a new land.

Amerigo Vespucci

Amerigo Vespucci was a banker and merchant who stocked ships with food and supplies. He was interested in exploring, and he claimed that he had a new system for steering ships. His method was probably not as good as he said it was—the pilots he tried to train wouldn't use it—but he became well known. He joined several voyages across the ocean, probably as a paid passenger, and wrote about his travels. Vespucci realized that the land Christopher Columbus had found was not Asia. In his writings he called it the "New World."

The Mapmakers' Mistake

Mapmakers used Vespucci's tales of his travels to change their maps. They began to draw a new land between Europe and Asia. One mapmaker named the new land America, for Amerigo Vespucci. He said that Vespucci had discovered the new world, so it should be named after him.

At first, people did not realize that the "New World" of Amerigo Vespucci was the place Columbus had found. By the time they realized that the two were the same, many maps had been printed. The mapmakers tried to take the credit back from Vespucci, but it was too late. Too many people had seen the maps. They called the new land by the name on the maps—*America*. And so half of the world was named after a man who doesn't really deserve the honor.

TIP: *Put each answer choice into the passage in place of the underlined word. Pick the one that makes sense there.*

1 In paragraph 3, the word imprecise means—

A careful

B old

C not exact

D lucky

TIP: *If you don't know the answer, find it in the passage before you look at the answer choices. Then pick the answer closest to what you found in the passage.*

2 Why did mapmakers name America for Amerigo Vespucci?

A He was the first to discover it.

B He was first to call it the "New World."

C He made the first map of it.

D He told people how to get to it.

TIP: *Be sure the answer you choose is the main idea, not just an important detail.*

3 What is the main idea of the section "Columbus's Discovery"?

A Some people thought the world was 25,000 miles around.

B Europeans forgot Leif Ericsson's discovery.

C Sailors looked for better ways to get where they wanted to go.

D Columbus's discovery was based on a mistake.

TIP: *The setting is often stated near the beginning, or you can use clues in the passage to help you figure it out.*

4 When did the events in this selection take place?

A Around the time of Leif Ericsson

B In modern times

C About 100 years ago

D Around the time of Columbus

TIP: *Facts can be looked up or proved, but opinions can't be. Look for opinion words to help you identify opinions.*

5 Which of the following is an OPINION expressed in the passage?

A Amerigo Vespucci was a banker.

B A mapmaker named the new land "America."

C The New World should not have been named after Amerigo Vespucci.

D Early maps showed only Europe, Asia, and Africa.

Sample Passage E

Pablo the Clown

Victor's mother met him at the door after school. "Your cousin Pablo is here," she said. "He hasn't been here since you were little. Come and meet him. Pablo works for the circus. He's a clown."

Victor followed his mother inside. There sat a small man with sparkling black eyes and a wide grin. He had on a shirt and slacks, and his hair was neatly combed. "Are you really a clown? You don't look like a clown," said Victor.

Pablo laughed and opened his big suitcase. Out of it spilled an orange jacket and a pair of purple pants. There was a green polka-dotted shirt and a flowered tie. "Oh, boy," said Victor. "Put them on!"

"Not so fast," said Pablo. "A real clown always puts on make-up before clothes. Would you like me to show you how?"

They went into the kitchen. On the table, Pablo spread out the things he needed to put on his clown face. There were tubes of make-up, brushes, baby powder, cotton, paper towels, a plastic shower cap, an apron, and a mirror. "Wow," said Victor. "You need all that?"

Pablo covered his hair with the shower cap and put on the apron. Then he spread white greasepaint on his face. He even covered his eyebrows. Next, he carefully wiped off the white makeup in spots. "Why are you doing that?" asked Victor.

"These are the spots where I will put my other makeup," explained Pablo. He powdered his face. "This sets the makeup so it won't come off," he said. Then he drew outlines of funny eyebrows on his forehead in black and filled them in with red. He outlined his eyes and painted the tip of his nose. He drew a wide mouth. He set each feature with powder. Then he took off the shower cap and put on a huge red wig. Victor laughed. Pablo really was a clown.

"Now you try it," said Pablo.

Victor put on the shower cap and dipped his fingers in the white greasepaint. He tried to spread it on his face the way Pablo had. At first he got too much in some places and not enough in others, but he decided it looked all right. He tried to wipe off spots where he wanted to paint new features. He wiped off too much, and had to start over.

At last Victor was ready to paint on his eyebrows, eyes, nose, and mouth. It was a lot harder than he thought! When he was done, one eyebrow was too high, one eye was bigger than the other, and his mouth was crooked. Pablo told him it was pretty good for a first try, though, so Victor decided it was OK.

While Victor was admiring his new face in the mirror, Pablo was rummaging in his suitcase. He pulled out a package. "This is for you," he said.

Victor tore it open. It was a clown suit and wig of his own. He started to put them on. "Now I'm really a clown too," he said.

"Not quite," said Pablo. "There are a few things you don't know. If you want to learn, we could start tomorrow. I'll teach you to juggle." Victor could hardly wait.

TIP: *Put each answer choice into the passage in place of the underlined word. Pick the one that makes sense there.*

1 In this passage, the word greasepaint means the same as—

A lotion

B soap

C makeup

D spots

TIP: *Compare the answer choices with the directions in the passage.*

2 To put on his clown face, which did Pablo do first?

A Spread on white makeup

B Put on a shower cap

C Powdered his face

D Put a red rubber ball on his nose

TIP: *Choose a summary that covers the whole passage and gives all the important facts.*

3 Which statement below is the best summary of the selection?

A Cousin Pablo, a clown, shows Victor his clown act.

B Victor meets his cousin Pablo, who is a clown, for the first time.

C Victor's cousin Pablo, a clown, shows him how to put on a clown's makeup.

D Victor learns all about how to be a clown.

TIP: *Look for an answer that seems logical and makes sense with the rest of the passage.*

4 Which of these things is Victor likely to do?

A Leave home and join the circus

B Make money by being a clown

C Learn how to juggle from Pablo

D Teach his mother how to apply clown makeup

TIP: *Look for clues in the passage. Check all the answers before you choose one.*

5 How does Victor feel at the end of the selection?

A Discouraged

B Excited

C Bored

D Tired

Sample Passage F

The First American Woman in Space

On June 18, 1983, the space shuttle *Challenger* blasted off from Florida's Cape Canaveral. On this trip, astronauts would use a new mechanical arm to capture items floating in space and bring them back into the ship for the first time. It would also carry the first doctor to study space sickness. These two "firsts" were important, but there was another "first" that everybody was talking about. On the crew was the first American woman in space—Sally Ride.

While Sally Ride was studying at Stanford University, she read an interesting ad. It said that the United States space agency, NASA, was looking for scientists who wanted to go into space. These scientists did not have to be pilots. They would perform scientific experiments in space. The ad also said women were welcome.

Sally Ride was studying physics, a branch of science. She would soon have her doctor's degree, and she would be looking for a job. She decided to apply to NASA. So did 5,680 other people, including 1,251 women. Thirty-five people were chosen. Six were women, and Dr. Sally Ride was one of them.

Sally Ride spent a year training to be an astronaut. She was ready to go into space. Very few astronauts can go into space at one time, however. Some never go. They have important jobs on the ground.

NASA assigned Sally Ride to help develop a robotic arm for the shuttle. The arm had to be able to grasp a satellite or other equipment that was floating in space and bring it back into the shuttle for repair or testing. The mechanical arm could also be used to put objects into space safely away from the spacecraft.

Sally Ride worked on the arm for three years. She did other jobs as well. Twice, she served as the communicator, or radio link, between a crew in space and the scientists on the ground. She helped to develop new programs for space exploration.

When the mechanical arm was ready, NASA had to choose a member of the team to test it in space. They chose Sally Ride. They said she was "the very best person for the job."

Sally Ride saw herself as an astronaut and a scientist, a part of the crew. The people of America, however, saw her as a role model who was doing something no American woman had ever done before. Television crews and newspaper reporters asked her questions about her feelings and thoughts. She said she planned to do the job she had been trained to do as well as she possibly could.

The mission lasted seven days. With Sally Ride at the controls, the mechanical arm performed perfectly. It was able to capture and release satellites in space. The mission was a great success. The first American woman in space insisted that she had done nothing special. She was just part of the team.

IMPORTANT DATES IN SALLY RIDE'S LIFE

1951 Born May 26 in Encino, California.

1973-1978 Graduates from Stanford University and receives a master's degree and doctor's degree in physics.

1977 Applies to the NASA astronaut program

1978 Selected as an astronaut

1979 Completes one-year astronaut training program.

1981 Communicator for space shuttle flight two and three, acting as radio link between the crew in space and the ground.

1982 Communicator for space shuttle flight three.

1983, June 18-24 Crew member on *Challenger* shuttle, the first American woman in space, the first astronaut to use new mechanical arm.

1984 Second flight on *Challenger*.

1987 Returns to teach at Stanford University.

TIP: *Put each answer choice into the passage in place of the underlined word. Pick the one that makes sense there.*

1 In this passage the word robotic means the same as—

A shuttle

B mechanical

C human

D satellite

TIP: *Try to find the answer in the passage before you look at the answer choices. Be sure that the event actually happened first.*

2 Which event in Sally Ride's life happened first?

A She became the first American woman in space.

B She answered a NASA advertisement.

C She developed a mechanical arm for the space program.

D She was communicator for two space flights.

TIP: *Be sure the answer you choose is the main idea, not just an important detail.*

3 What statement best expresses the main idea of the sixth paragraph?

A Sally Ride did a variety of jobs at NASA.

B Sally Ride served as a communicator.

C Sally Ride developed a mechanical arm.

D Sally Ride waited patiently for her turn to go into space.

TIP: *Be sure you can find the detail in the passage.*

4 The *Challenger* mission of June 18, 1983, attracted special attention because—

A it carried a doctor to study space sickness

B it was the first trip of the space shuttle

C it was testing the mechanical arm

D it carried a woman

TIP: *Look for ideas and information in the reading passage to support your answer.*

5 Sally Ride was chosen to go into space because—

A she was a woman

B she was the best person to test the mechanical arm

C it was her turn

D she was the only astronaut who knew physics

TIP: *Check the time line before you choose your answer. Don't just look at the answer choices.*

6 According to the time line, in what year was Sally Ride selected to be an astronaut?

A 1977

B 1978

C 1982

D 1983

Sample Passage G

George Washington Carver and the Riddle of the Peanut

The great African-American scientist George Washington Carver worked and taught in a small college in Tuskegee, Alabama, around 1900. Carver's special interest was plants. He wanted to use his knowledge of plants to help the poor farmers of the South have a better life.

In the farms around Tuskegee, almost everybody grew cotton, nothing but cotton. Carver showed his students how to grow healthier plants that produced more cotton. Soon, Carver's fame spread. When farmers had a problem with their crops, they turned to him for help.

Then a really serious problem came along. It was a little beetle called a boll weevil, which ate cotton. The weevils spread all across the South from Texas to Florida, eating as they went and destroying the cotton crop. Not even Carver could stop the weevil. The only solution was to grow something weevils would not eat.

Carver suggested the peanut. Peanuts grew well in Alabama and were good to eat. Still, a problem remained. If all the farmers followed his advice, there would be a lot of peanuts—tons and tons. What would people do with all those peanuts?

Carver's training in science had taught him how to solve a problem. First, he knew, he had to take it apart. Then he had to look at each part. Finally he had to recombine the parts—put them together again, but in new ways or with other things to make something entirely new. The peanuts were Carver's problem.

In his laboratory, Carver shelled some peanuts, putting the shells in one pile and the papery skins in another. He put the nuts in a press and squeezed them until oil began to drip from them. For weeks, Carver experimented with the oil. He discovered that it mixed well with other things and was good to cook with. It could also be used in other products that were made with oil, like paint, ink, and soap.

Carver was not done. He mixed the powdery bits of nut that were left with water and made "milk." From the skin that covered the nuts, he made paper. From the shells, he made boards. Altogether, Carver made over three hundred different products from peanuts. You probably eat one of them—peanut butter. Soon people were building factories to make the products Carver had invented.

Carver did not stop with the peanut. He made marble from sawdust and rubber from sweet potatoes. He made dyes from many different kinds of plants. Using parts of plants as Carver did had never been done before. In doing them, Carver created a whole new branch of science, called chemurgy. It is the science of making products from plants.

1 In this passage, the word <u>recombine</u> means—

A put back together

B fix

C take apart

D change

2 The first step in solving a scientific problem is—

A to make something new

B to take the problem apart

C to examine part of the problem

D to put the parts together

3 Which statement below is the best summary of this passage?

A George Washington Carver was a teacher from Alabama.

B George Washington Carver was a famous scientist.

C George Washington Carver used his science skills to find new uses for the peanut and other plants.

D George Washington Carver was able to make almost anything.

4 What caused the cotton crop to fail?

A The boll weevil ate it.

B The farmers did not know how to grow it.

C The plants were not healthy.

D Carver told the farmers to plant peanuts.

5 When Carver first faced the problem of the peanut, he probably felt—

A concerned and anxious

B angry

C proud

D sad and lonely

6 Which statement best tells where the story takes place?

A In a modern laboratory

B On a farm in the 1800's

C In a cotton field many years ago

D In Alabama around 1900

Sample Passage H

Where Do We Get Our Oil?

Oil, or petroleum, is a natural resource. It comes from deep in the earth. People search for oil by drilling through many layers of earth and rock. Far underground, they may find a pool of oil, which they bring to the surface to use for fuel and other products.

How Does Oil Get Underground?

How did the oil get underground in the first place? Where oil occurs, scientists believe that there was once ocean. The ocean was full of plants and tiny animals. These creatures died and sank to the bottom.

Over long periods of time, layers of mud, sand and rock settled to the bottom and covered the ocean creatures. No oxygen could reach them, so they did not rot away. As more layers built up, the older layers hardened, forming rock. The oceans dried up, and the creatures that once swam in them were buried under tons of rock.

The pressure from the rock caused the creatures to change. Slowly, they changed into oil. The drops of oil ran together through cracks in the rock to form pools.

How Do We Get Oil?

Getting oil out of the ground is a big job. Scientists look for oil by studying maps and drilling test holes. When they find a likely spot, workers drill through the rock hoping to find a pool of oil. They use pumps to bring the oil to the surface. The oil they find, called crude oil, is not ready to use. It must first go to a refinery, a place that cleans it and makes it into different oil products.

How Do We Use Oil?

We use petroleum in many important ways. Heating oil for homes comes from petroleum. Gasoline for cars, trucks, airplanes, and other machinery comes from petroleum. Some house paint is made from petroleum. Plastic is a petroleum product, and so is nylon. Petroleum jelly or baby oil are in many medicine chests. There are too many products made with oil to list.

Why Save Oil?

The oil we are using today was formed a very long time ago. We use oil much faster than the earth can make it. Some oil fields have already run dry. Scientists are searching for other sources of energy. Until they succeed, one of the best things to do is to try to save the oil we have by saving energy at home.

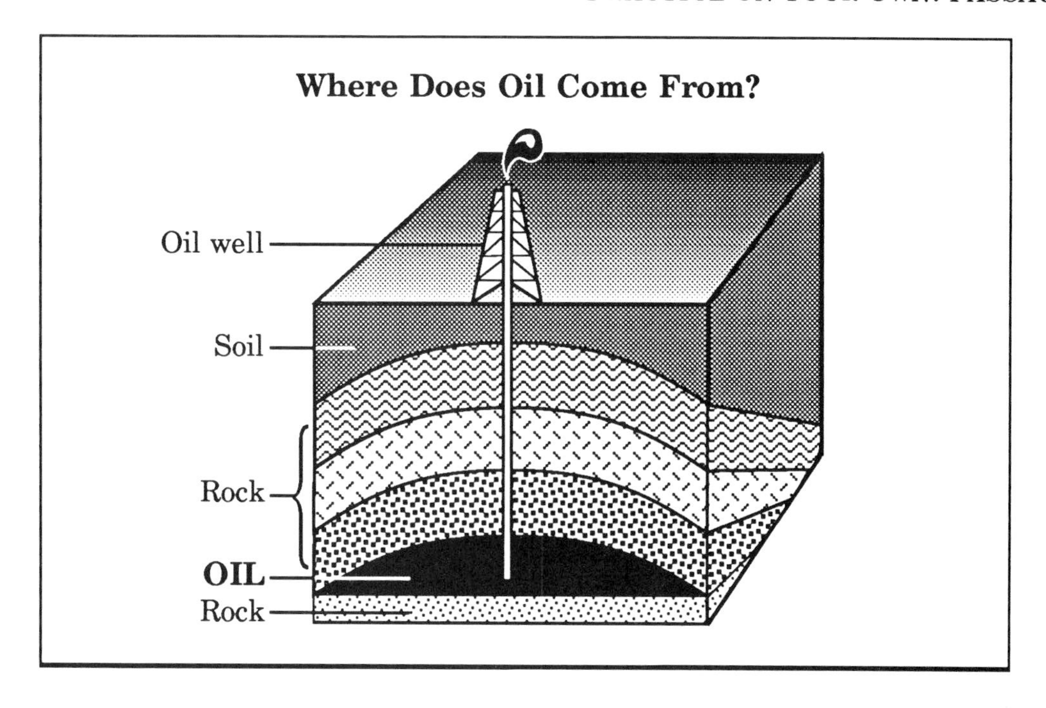

1 In this passage, <u>petroleum</u> means the same as—

A medicine
B oil
C resource
D fuel

2 What happened before layers of mud settled on the ocean floor?

A The layers turned into rock.
B The oceans dried up.
C Tiny animals sank to the bottom of the ocean.
D Oil formed pools.

3 What is the main idea of paragraph 6?

A Heating oil comes from petroleum.
B There are too many products made from oil.
C House paint, plastic, and nylon are petroleum products.
D We use petroleum in many important ways.

4 What might happen to the oil supply in the future?

A The earth will make more.
B It will probably increase.
C We won't need it any more.
D It will probably be used up.

5 According to the diagram, what is the layer just above oil in the ground?

A soil
B rock
C ocean creatures
D ocean bottom

Sample Passage I

Why Are Scientists Studying Parrots?

Would you like to own a parrot? People have kept parrots as pets for many hundreds of years. Parrots seem to like people. They often become attached to their owners. They can also learn to talk. People have always believed that parrots are very smart birds.

Can Parrots Think?

Scientists are studying parrots to find out just how smart they really are. One scientist, Dr. Irene Pepperberg, has a parrot named Alex that can talk. Dr. Pepperberg has taught Alex to recognize colors, shapes, and simple objects like paper, wood, keys, and boxes.

Saying what color or shape something is seems easy for Alex, and he can do even harder things. If Dr. Pepperberg asks Alex "What object is red?" Alex can say "the box." This question is harder because Alex must do two things—he must both know the color and recognize the object.

Alex appears to understand the question and put ideas together to come up with the answer. Some scientists believe this ability shows that Alex is thinking. Other scientists are not sure that Alex really thinks, but they agree that he is a very unusual bird.

What About Wild Parrots?

Scientists studying wild parrots have noticed that most parrot pairs remain together for life. Even when they are not raising young, pairs remain together and seem to show affection, cuddling and preening each other's feathers. Families may stay together until the young are fully grown and find mates of their own. Parents teach their young. Young parrots from different families may also get together for play and lessons from older parrots.

Why Study Parrots Now?

Scientists feel that now may be their last chance to find out about parrots. For one thing, the parrots' habitat is shrinking. Every year, the area where they live gets smaller as people cut down the trees where they build their nests. Perhaps because there are fewer places to nest, parrots do not raise a family every year. When they do nest, they lay only two eggs. Often, only one baby parrot lives. Moreover, when hunters capture rare parrots to sell, the parrots die in cages. Finally, some native people shoot parrots to eat or to get feathers for decorations.

Scientists are trying to convince people in areas where parrots live that these colorful creatures are more valuable alive than dead. They hope that these beautiful, interesting birds will be around for a long time to come.

1 In this passage, <u>habitat</u> means—

A place where something lives

B behavior

C jungle

D way of doing things

2 What kind of question appears hardest for Alex?

A Identifying the shapes of objects

B Identifying objects by name

C Identifying colors

D Identifying an object of a particular color

3 What main idea is implied in in paragraph 5?

A Scientists are studying wild parrots as well as tame ones.

B Parrot families are like human families in many ways.

C Mother parrots make good parents.

D Young parrots often get together to play.

4 Why do scientists feel they should study parrots now?

A Parrots are the only smart birds there are.

B In the future, people will not be interested in parrots.

C Talking parrots can tell scientists things.

D Parrots are in danger of disappearing.

5 Which of the following statements is an OPINION expressed in the passage?

A Alex is thinking when he answers a question.

B Parrots can learn to talk.

C The area where parrots nest is getting smaller.

D Hunters capture parrots to sell.

Sample Passage J

How Did Peter Solve His Problem?

Peter was afraid it was going to be a very boring summer. Most of his friends were away at camp. His mother and father both worked all day. His sister had a job, too. Peter had spent the past two days looking for a job for himself. He got the same answer everywhere. "You're too young," they'd say. "Come back in a few years." One woman told him he was "unemployable" because of his age.

Peter wanted to keep busy. He wanted to earn some money of his own. He had even decided what he'd like to do. He wanted to work with animals. Peter had tried every pet shop and animal doctor in town, but nobody wanted him, not even as a volunteer.

He was sitting on the porch watching people walking down the street when Dr. Kurtz came by with her dog, Lulu. Lulu was tugging at her leash and Dr. Kurtz was toting a big animal carrier. It looked heavy. Just as they got to Peter's house, she put it down.

"Could I carry that for you?" Peter asked.

"Yes, thank you, Peter," Dr. Kurtz said. "That's very nice of you." Peter picked up the carrier and they started off again. "I'm going on vacation," Dr. Kurtz explained. "The carrier is so I can take Lulu to the dog kennel so she'll be taken care of when I'm gone. I hate to do it—Lulu doesn't like the kennel."

Peter heard himself saying, "I could take care of Lulu. You could leave her at home."

"You'd have to walk her four times a day and feed her and clean up after her," Dr. Kurtz said.

"I'd do it for pay," Peter said. "A job. Pet sitting. I'd be cheaper than the kennel. And Lulu would be happier."

"Well," said Dr. Kurtz, "it's a lot of work. Lulu gets a long walk before her breakfast. Then she has her biggest meal. Before she eats, she has to have her pill. She gets a short walk around noon. Then around four o'clock, she has another long walk and play. She gets a biscuit after that. She needs a big bowl of fresh water every time she walks. Finally, she gets a short walk before bed."

"I could do that," said Peter.

They had reached Dr. Kurtz's house. "I'll think about it," she said, "and let you know."

Peter raced home and went to work. When his mother came home, he showed her the sign he had made.

PETE'S PET CARE

DOG WALKING, FEEDING, BATHING

DOG AND CAT SITTING

FISH AND HAMSTER CARE
IN MY HOME

Pet lover will take care of
your pet while you're away.

REASONABLE RATES

Call 555-4283

Just then the phone rang. "It's for Pete," his sister called. "It's Dr. Kurtz."

"Hello," Peter said. "Pete's Pet Care."

"I've decided to take you up on your offer," Dr. Kurtz told him. "I think Lulu would be much happier with you taking care of her." They agreed on a fee and set up a time for him to learn about Lulu's care. Peter was very pleased.

His mother was still admiring his sign. "This looks like a really good idea," she said. "Tomorrow we'll get copies for you to hang up in some of the stores."

"Great," said Peter."And guess what? I've already got my first customer!"

1 In this passage, the word unemployable means—

A young

B able to be used

C not able to be hired for work

D not making a profit

2 What must Peter do just before he gives Lulu her breakfast?

A give her water

B take her for a short walk

C give her a pill

D clean up after her

3 Which of these is the best summary for this passage?

A Peter finds something to do for the summer.

B Lulu the dog gets to stay home while Dr. Kurtz goes on vacation.

C Peter decides to become a pet care specialist and makes a sign advertising his services.

D Peter realizes that he can get work taking care of pets and gets Lulu as his first customer.

4 Which animals will Peter care for in his home?

A dogs

B hamsters

C cats

D birds

5 Which of the following statements is a FACT stated in the passage?

A Peter will do a good job taking care of Lulu.

B Lulu likes the kennel.

C Lulu needs water.

D Peter's rates are reasonable.

Sample Passage K

The Rio Grande

The longest river in Texas, the Rio Grande is also one of the major rivers of the Southwest. It begins in the mountains of Colorado and flows through the state of New Mexico. Then it turns east to form the border between Texas and Mexico. By the time it empties into the Gulf of Mexico, the giant river is shallow and sluggish. Near its beginning, however, the Rio Grande runs fast and wild and free.

What Is a Wild and Scenic River?

In 1968, Congress passed the Wild and Scenic Rivers Act. This law protects parts of American rivers from things like buildings, dams, motor boats, and pollution. Forty-eight miles of the Rio Grande in northern New Mexico is protected as a Wild and Scenic River. There, the river flows through a deep, narrow valley. It rushes quickly over rocks and waterfalls, creating rough water called "rapids." This part of the river is called "The Grand Canyon of the Rio Grande."

River Activities

At times when the river is high, many people bring small boats like kayaks and rafts and paddle down the river. One popular and exciting sport on this part of the Rio Grande is "white water" boating. White-water boaters paddle through the rapids, which are called "white water" because of the bubbles around the rocks. White-water kayaking or rafting requires skill and courage. The person steering the boat must be able to control it around rocks and over small waterfalls.

Some visitors fish in river pools for different kinds of fish. Still other people may hike on along the trails. The area around the river is full of wild flowers, trees, butterflies, and interesting rocks for people to study and enjoy. They can camp, swim, or picnic. They can also stop at the Visitors' Center to learn about the history of the area and how the river formed the valley. Many people go to the area just to see the beautiful scenery.

Native Americans and the Rio Grande

Parts of the Grand Canyon of the Rio Grande are sacred to the Native American tribes that live nearby. Local tribe members come to the river to gather red willow, a plant that is used for making baskets and in other special ways, such as for medicine.

The Way to the Gulf

After it leaves the canyon, the river flows more slowly. It makes its way down through New Mexico and along the Texas border. It makes a huge, sweeping curve to form the big bend of Big Bend National Park, home to many rare birds and plants. By the time the Rio Grande reaches the Gulf of Mexico, it has traveled 1,800 miles through mountains and desert, valleys and flat plains to reach the sea.

1 In this passage, the word sluggish means—

A slow-moving
B deep
C fast-moving
D wide

2 What is the Grand Canyon of the Rio Grande?

A The area around Big Bend National Park
B The border between Texas and Mexico
C A deep river valley in New Mexico
D Part of Colorado

3 What is the main idea of the fourth paragraph?

A Many visitors fish in the river.
B People come to the river for the scenery.
C The Visitors' Center helps people decide what to do.
D A visitor can do many things besides boating.

4 What is the cause of "white water"?

A pollution
B air bubbles
C white dust in the water
D boaters

5 Why is white-water boating popular only when the river is high?

A There is nothing else to do then.
B The water is deep enough then.
C The boat is easier to control then.
D More people bring their boats then.

Sample Passage L

Barbara Jordan

Barbara Jordan always wanted to do something outstanding with her life. In 1972, she achieved that goal when Texans chose her to run for United States Congress. More than eighty percent of the voters in her district voted for her. She was elected easily. The election made history, because Barbara Jordan was the first African-American Congresswoman ever elected to the United States House of Representatives from a Southern state.

Barbara Jordan grew up in Houston. At first, she did not know what she would be, but one day a woman lawyer came to the school to describe her work. After hearing her speak, Barbara decided that she, too, would be a lawyer.

After going to law school in the East, she set up a law practice in Houston. She also became interested in politics and decided to run for the Texas State Legislature. There had not been an African-American in the Texas House of Representatives for nearly a hundred years. Many people believed that an African-American woman could never be elected, but Barbara Jordan did not let that stop her. She had been brought up to believe she could be anything she wanted to be.

The first time she ran for office, she lost. Two years later, she ran again—and lost again. She thought of leaving Texas, but she had received over 60,000 votes. Because all those people had voted for her, she decided she should keep trying. Three years later, she ran for the state senate. By that time, changes in national and state laws had made it easier for people to vote. Barbara Jordan won. She went to Austin as the only African-American member of the Texas Senate.

In her first year in the senate, Barbara Jordan's fellow senators named her the outstanding new senator of that year. She was a brilliant speaker and a successful lawmaker. The senate often voted for the legislation she suggested. As one of the Texas Senate's most highly respected members, she won a second term easily.

After two terms in Texas, Barbara Jordan was ready to move on. The voters sent her to Washington as their Congresswoman. In Congress, she worked to pass laws that would help education, health care, and the poor. One of her duties was to serve on the committee that looked into the actions of President Richard Nixon when he was accused of doing wrong.

Barbara Jordan left Congress when her term was up and returned to Texas. She said she did not want to run for office again. Instead, she started teaching government and politics. As usual, she wanted to be outstanding—the very best college teacher she could be. She worked as hard at being a teacher as she did at being a Congresswoman.

Recently, Texas Governor Ann Richards needed someone to help her make sure that the people who work for her in the government are honest and fair. She asked Barbara Jordan to take the job. So Barbara Jordan went back into government again. Although she is not old, she sometimes walks with a cane or uses a wheelchair because of illness. However, she does not let that stop her. Barbara Jordan is still determined to be outstanding at anything she does.

1 In this passage the word legislation means—

A money
B laws
C advice
D legal papers

2 What did Barbara Jordan do after her term in the Texas Senate?

A She went to law school.
B She ran for the U.S. Congress.
C She ran for the Texas House of Representatives.
D She set up a law practice in Houston.

3 Where did Barbara Jordan work when she was in the Texas Senate?

A Houston
B Washington
C Austin
D The East

4 What is the main idea of this passage?

A Barbara Jordan was a Texas Congresswoman.
B Barbara Jordan was the first African-American elected to Congress.
C Barbara Jordan was determined to be outstanding and has succeeded.
D Barbara Jordan is still working in government.

5 Which of these is Barbara Jordan most likely to do next?

A Run for President
B Complete her job in an outstanding way
C Become the head of a rich law firm
D Leave Texas

6 When Barbara Jordan lost in her second race for state representative, she probably felt—

A angry and hurt
B cheerful and amused
C bored and uninterested
D proud and outstanding

SECTION B
WRITING, PART 1
WRITTEN COMPOSITION

B: WRITTEN COMPOSITION SECTION GUIDE TO THE TEACHER

This part of the TAAS Coach introduces students to the general requirements of writing a composition for the TAAS test. It then takes the students through five lessons, one for each of the five types of writing that may be tested on the composition portion of the TAAS test.

Each of the composition lessons contains four sections. The first two sections consist of two kinds of instruction:

1. ***Improving the Composition*** uses guided revision to instruct students in the elements of a successful TAAS composition. The revising can be done either as a group activity or as an individual activity. If done as a group activity, responses can be oral. If done individually, students should write their responses.

   Use the group approach for a quick review of any of the types of writing. The individual approach permits more intensive teaching of a particular type of composition.

2. ***Writing Your Own Composition,*** as the title says, has students write their own compositions in response to a prompt given in the text.

3. ***After You Write*** gives students an opportunity for collaborative learning as students share their compositions with each other. The questions in this section guide students through peer response to these shared compositions. They also guide the authors of the compositions in revising what they have written.

4. ***Keeping in Shape,*** the final section, contains extension activities that can be used throughout the year to develop the critical thinking skills that are the foundation of good writing.

B: WRITTEN COMPOSITION SECTION GUIDE TO THE STUDENT

KINDS OF COMPOSITION

One part of the TAAS Writing test tests how well you can write a composition. The test makers will pick one out of these five types of composition for you to write:

1. ***A descriptive composition.*** (You may be asked to describe something that is in a picture.)
2. ***A how-to composition.*** (You may be asked to tell how you do something—for example, how you clean your teeth.)
3. ***A narrative composition, or story.*** (You may be asked to tell a story about something that is happening in a picture.)
4. ***A composition about the good points and bad points of something.*** (For example, you might be asked to write about the good and bad points of doing your homework right away when you get home.)
5. ***A persuasive composition.*** (For example, you might be asked if you would rather live in the city or the country. You would have to write a composition explaining your reasons for your choice.)

Even though you will only write one composition for the test, you need to practice writing all five.

THINGS YOU MAY WANT TO KNOW

Is there any special information I need in order to write a TAAS composition?

No. You don't need to know any special facts.

It helps to be a good observer and to be aware of what is going on around you. For example, are there any problems or issues that students are concerned about in your school? Are there activities or hobbies that you do? All these may be useful when you write the composition for this test.

How long does my composition have to be?

Usually, you will be able to do a satisfactory job in three or four paragraphs.

How much time do I have?

As much as you need. The test is not timed.

Should I spend time making prewriting notes or an outline?

Prewriting is not graded, but it will help you write a better essay and get a better score. Use the space provided to list ideas, jot down notes, or make a web or an outline.

Does neatness count?

Of course, if no one can read your composition, it can't be scored at all. But the test-graders mainly want to know how well you write, not how neatly you write.

HOW IS MY COMPOSITION GRADED?

- ***0 is the lowest grade.*** It is a composition that cannot be scored. The paper is blank, or the handwriting is too messy to read, or the composition is written in another language. A composition that is about another topic altogether will also get a 0.
- ***1 is an unsatisfactory composition.*** It is usually too short, poorly organized, and filled with errors.
- ***2 is barely satisfactory.*** It has some organization and elaboration but needs more. (You'll learn about elaboration in the next section.)
- ***3 is a successful composition.*** It is fairly well developed and organized. There are no major errors in spelling, usage, or punctuation.
- ***4 is the highest score.*** It is an excellent composition—clear, complete, well organized, and fully elaborated.

If your composition is given a 0 or a 1, there is no way you can pass the writing test, no matter how well you do on the other part of the writing test. If your composition is a 2, you will need a superior score on the rest of the test to pass. Someone who scores a 3 or 4 on the composition usually passes.

WHAT TEST GRADERS LOOK FOR

GENERAL QUALITIES

Your composition will be scored on how clear, complete, and well organized it is. Small mistakes like misspelled words or misplaced commas will not count very much. Instead, the test graders look for the following things. Make these the targets you aim for.

1. ***Elaboration.*** Elaboration means developing each of your ideas fully. When you write your own composition, make sure that you elaborate as completely as possible. More students fail the test because they have not elaborated enough than for any other reason.

2. ***Organization.*** Organization means arranging things in an order that makes sense. A well-organized essay also uses words and phrases that make its order clear to the reader.

3. ***Language Control.*** Language control means expressing yourself effectively, clearly, and correctly. You need well-constructed sentences, varied and correct word choice, and as few errors as possible.

4. ***Awareness of Audience.*** Remember that you have to describe or explain things so completely and clearly that your reader can understand them, too.

SPECIFIC QUALITIES

In addition to these general characteristics of a good composition, test graders look for the following specific points.

A DESCRIPTIVE COMPOSITION

- Does ***not*** tell a story
- Describes one thing completely before moving on to the next
- Uses words that help the reader see the picture

A HOW-TO COMPOSITION

- Gives the steps in order
- Tells how to do each step fully before moving on to the next
- Uses words that help the reader know what to do

A NARRATIVE COMPOSITION

- Has a clear beginning and ending
- Tells about the events in the order in which they happen
- Uses words that help the reader see what is happening

A COMPOSITION ABOUT GOOD AND BAD POINTS

- Discusses both the good points and the bad points of something
- Organizes the good points and the bad points separately
- Uses words that help the reader understand exactly what the good points and bad points are

A PERSUASIVE COMPOSITION

- Takes a clear position
- Supports the position with good reasons
- Uses facts, examples, explanations, and personal experience to elaborate the reasons
- Appeals to the reader

HOW TO READ THE PROMPT

Your first job when you write a TAAS composition is to make sure that you understand the prompt—the question you have been asked to write about.

STEP 1
READ THE PROMPT

- What is my first response to the prompt?
- Do I have any ideas about what I want to say?

STEP 2
IDENTIFY THE TASK

- What am I supposed to write about?
- Who is my reader?

STEP 3
USE WHAT YOU KNOW

- What experiences of my own can I use when I elaborate my ideas?

STEP 4
MAKE SOME PREWRITING NOTES

- Can I web, cluster, map, or chart my ideas?

Step 5
READ THE PROMPT AGAIN

- Have I covered everything? Am I ready to write?

When you have finished these steps, you will have done your prewriting. You will be ready to write your composition.

LESSON B1 THE DESCRIPTIVE COMPOSITION

This section will help you write a descriptive composition by—

- showing you how to revise a low-level composition
- guiding you through the writing of your own composition
- suggesting additional ways to prepare for writing descriptions

THE DESCRIPTIVE COMPOSITION

Here is a prompt that asks you to write a description:

> On the following page is a picture of an elephant who has a lot to eat. Look at the picture and write a composition for your teacher in which you describe what you see.

Here is the composition one student wrote.

> I am going to describe a picture that our teacher gave us. This elephant is big and gray. There is a tree as tall as the Empire State building with leaves like caterpillars. The elephant is tied up. There is a rope on a little stick. And a bucket with the word Water on it. And there is a big square of hay. There are piles of vegetables in front of the tent they are for the elephant to eat. The elephant has a trunk and two tusks and two eyes. He is saying to himself, "I can eat everything I see." I think his name should be Greedy. I see fruit and vegetables and I see lots of bread. There are carrots, apples, pears, cabbages, bananas, potatoes, corn, watermelon, and French bread and regular bread. My ending is that is my description of the elephant.

WATER

This composition did not receive a passing score. Can you tell why? Look back at "What Test Graders Look For" in the Section Guide. Then write one reason that you think this composition did not pass.

____

____

IMPROVING THE COMPOSITION

Here are some questions that good writers ask themselves when they revise a composition like this one. Pretend that you wrote this composition. In the blanks following each question, write the changes you would make in the composition.

1. In a description, I should begin by telling the reader what my composition is about. Have I done this? If not, how should I begin? (*HINT:* The prompt will often tell you what the picture shows.)

____

____

2. I should describe all the important things in the picture. Have I described everything in the picture? If not, what do I need to add?

____

____

3. I need to describe things in some kind of order. For example, have I kept all the details about the elephant together? Have I kept all the details about the food together? If not, what do I need to change?

____

____

4. I need to tell my reader where things are. For example, I need to say what is on the right, what is on the left, what is in front, what is in back, and so on. Have I done this? If not, what do I need to add?

____

____

5. I also need to give my reader enough details so that he or she can see the picture as clearly as I do. For example, have I said what the elephant is doing with his trunk or where the scene takes place? If not, what do I need to add?

____

____

6. The details I use must be specific. For example, I need to say exactly what things look like. I need to use my imagination to say what they are made of, how big they are, what colors they are, and so on. Have I done this? If not, what do I need to add?

____

____

7. I must remember that I am writing a description, NOT telling a story. The details I give must tell how things look, not what might happen in the picture. Are there any details that do not belong? If so, what should I take out?

____

____

8. When I use a comparison to show what something looks like, it has to make sense. Have I done this? If not, what do I need to change?

____

____

9. I need to end my composition by saying something about the picture. Have I done this? If not, what do I need to change?

___

___

10. I need to write complete sentences. Have I avoided fragments and run-ons? If not, what changes should I make?

___

___

WRITING YOUR OWN COMPOSITION

Here is a new prompt that asks you to write a descriptive composition. Notice that this prompt does not have a picture for you to describe. Instead it asks you to tell about something you are familiar with.

> Think of a room in your house or apartment. It could be the kitchen, the living room, the room where you sleep. Write a composition for a friend in which you describe this room. Include detailsthat will help your friend see the room clearly.

Read the prompt again, and answer these questions:

1. What rooms are there in my house or apartment?

___

___

2. Which room can I describe easily and in detail to someone else?

___

___

3. What do I want to say first about this room? Can I say something that will give my reader a general impression of the room? (To help you answer this question, close your eyes and see the room you are describing.)

____

____

4. I can describe the most important part of the room first. Or I can move from one side of the room to another. Or I can begin by describing what I see first when I walk into the room, and then what I see next. Where do I want to begin my description?

____

____

5. I need to give my reader enough details so that he or she can see the room as clearly as I do. These details need to be specific. For example, I need to say what things are made of, what colors they are, and where they are located. (Close your eyes and visualize the room again.)

   The 1st thing I want to describe:

____

____

   The 2nd thing I want to describe:

____

____

   The 3rd thing I want to describe:

____

____

The rest of the things I want to describe:

____

____

____

____

6. I need to be sure that I have said enough. Do I want to add anything? Do I want to describe anything in greater detail?

____

____

7. I need to be sure that I have not told a story. Have I stuck to description, or have I told about things that happen in the room I am describing? Do I want to change anything?

____

____

8. What can I say at the end to show my reader that this composition is complete?

____

____

When you have answered these questions, you have done the prewriting and planning for your composition.

Now look at the chart on the next page. Here is another way to plan what you are going to write.

- Make a chart like this one and use it to help you write.
- On a separate sheet of paper, write the composition you have just planned.

DESCRIPTIVE COMPOSITION
PREWRITING

OBJECT 1:

Size ______________________________

Color ______________________________

Material ______________________________

Location ______________________________

Other Details ______________________________

____

OBJECT 2:

Size ______________________________

Color ______________________________

Material ______________________________

Location ______________________________

Other Details ______________________________

____

OBJECT 3:

Size ______________________________

Color ______________________________

Material ______________________________

Location ______________________________

Other Details ______________________________

____

WRITING A SECOND COMPOSITION

You may want to practice writing another descriptive composition. Here is a prompt that uses the picture on the next page:

> On the next page is a picture of two people who are riding horses on a ranch. Look at the picture and describe what you see. Write your description for a classmate to read.

When you write this composition, remember the following tips:

- Look carefully at the picture. Include everything you see in your description.
- Tell where things are in the picture—on the left, on the right, in front of, in back of.
- Use specific words that tell about size, shape, color, and so on.
- Remember that you are describing something. You are not telling a story.

AFTER YOU WRITE

Exchange papers with a classmate or share what you have written with a small group of students.

Ask yourself these questions when you read or listen to your classmates' compositions:

- What are some of the things I like in this composition?
- What are some of the things I would like to know more about?
- What are some of the things I would like the writer to explain?

KEEPING IN SHAPE

Here are some other ways to get ready for writing the TAAS descriptive composition.

1. Make a list of words that tell where things are located. Here are a few to start you off:

   beside

   in front of

   behind

2. Look at something in your classroom (for example, your teacher's desk) or something you can see from the window. Write down all the things you would include in a descriptive composition.

3. Close your eyes and think of someone you know well and like. Describe what you see to a classmate. Do NOT use the following words in your description:

   nice

   pretty

   interesting

   okay

Instead, tell what makes the person you are describing "nice" or "pretty" or "interesting."

LESSON B2
THE NARRATIVE COMPOSITION

This section will help you write a story, or narrative, by—

- showing you how to revise a low-level composition
- guiding you through the writing of your own composition
- suggesting additional ways to prepare for writing narratives

THE STORY

Here is a prompt that asks you to write a story.

> This is a picture of two children who are going trick-or-treating. Write a story for your teacher about what happens when the door to this house opens and the children walk in.

Here is the composition one student wrote.

> One Halloween there were these two kids knocking at the door of a house. One was named Todd he was dressed as a space monster. He had a head as big as a giant rock and giant hands as purple as grapes. His shoes were black with three glow-in-the-dark stripes on them. And there were silver things sticking out of his head. The other kid was Nikki. She was a witch with a broomstick and a tall hat. Then suddenly the door opened. "Let's go in," said Todd. "Is there anybody home?" called Nikki. When they went inside the house, they couldn't see anything it was too dark. Todd tripped on something. "What happened?" said Nikki. "I tripped on something," said Todd. Then out popped a skeleton. With only one

TRICK
OR
TREAT

> leg. Nikki reached down. There was a leg bone on the floor. The skeleton disappeared. "Let's get out of here," they said.

This composition did not receive a passing score. Can you tell why? Look at "What Test Graders Look For" in the Section Guide. Then write one reason that you think this composition did not pass.

____

____

IMPROVING THE COMPOSITION

Here are some questions good writers ask themselves when they revise a composition like this one. In the blanks following each question, write the changes you would make in this composition.

1. A good story has an interesting beginning. Do I have a beginning that makes the reader want to find out what happens next? If not, how should I begin?

____

____

2. A good story emphasizes action, not description. Have I fallen into the trap of describing too many things that are unimportant to the action of the story? If so, what do I need to change?

____

____

3. In a good story, the characters face a difficulty or problem of some kind. The story is about how they solve their problem. Do I have a problem or struggle in my story? Is the problem solved? If not, what do I need to add or change?

____

____

4. The action of the story needs to be clear. Can the reader understand everything that is happening in my story? Are there any things that still need to be explained? If so, what are they?

____

____

5. A good story does more than name the actions. It tells how things happen and why they happen. Does my story do this? If not, what do I need to add?

____

____

6. The language of a good story helps the reader see what is happening. Are the words I have used vivid and striking? If not, what do I need to change?

____

____

7. In a good story, the dialogue adds action to the plot. It does not repeat something that has already happened. Does my dialogue add action to the plot? If not, what do I need to change?

____

____

8. A good story does not just stop. The ending tells what happened to the characters or how they solved their problem. Does my story end this way? If not, what changes do I need to make?

____

____

9. Have I written complete sentences? Have I avoided fragments and run-ons? If not, what changes should I make?

____

____

WRITING YOUR OWN COMPOSITION

Here is a new prompt that asks you to write a narrative composition. Notice that this prompt does not have a picture for you to tell a story about. Instead it describes a scene and asks you to imagine what might happen.

> Rosa has just received a postcard telling her that she has won an unusual prize in a contest. She has to go to the zoo to pick it up. Write a story for a friend. Tell what happens to Rosa when she goes to get her prize.

Read the prompt again, and answer these questions:

1. What do I want my story to be about? (Close your eyes and visualize the scene described in the prompt. Try to see what happens to Rosa on the way to the zoo, what her prize is, and what happens after she picks up the prize.)

____

____

2. What is the prize? (Remember that the prompt says the prize is unusual. *HINT:* It's at the zoo.)

____

____

3. What problem or difficulty does Rosa face because of the prize?

____

____

4. Who else is in the story besides Rosa? What are their names? What are they like? What part do they play in the story?

____

____

5. How does Rosa solve her problem?

____

____

6. Where can I use dialogue to tell part of the story?

____

____

7. Where will I need to explain things to make the actions in my story clear?

____

____

8. What kind of beginning will make my reader want to find out what happens next?

____

____

9. What can I say at the end to show my reader that the story is complete?

____

____

When you have anwered these questions, you have done the prewriting and planning for your composition. On the next page is another way to plan what you are going to write.

NARRATIVE COMPOSITION
PREWRITING

CHARACTERS:

SETTING:

PROBLEM:

WHAT HAPPENS FIRST?

WHAT HAPPENS NEXT?

WHAT ELSE HAPPENS?

HOW DOES THE STORY END?

- Make a chart like this one and use it to help you write.
- On a separate sheet of paper, write the composition you have just planned.

WRITING A SECOND COMPOSITION

You may want to practice writing another story. Here is a prompt that uses a picture.

> On the following page is a picture of an astronaut who has just met some aliens. Write a story telling what happens when the astronaut explores this new planet. Write your story for a good friend to read.

When you write this composition, remember the following tips:

- The picture will help you begin your story. Look at the picture and try to see what will happen next.
- Decide who the other characters in the story are and what they are like.
- Figure out what problems or difficulties the characters will face.
- Decide how these problems will be solved.
- Use dialogue to tell part of the story.

AFTER YOU WRITE

Exchange papers with a classmate or share what you have written with a small group of students. Ask yourself these questions when you read or listen to your classmates' compositions:

- What are some of the things I like in this composition?
- What are some of the things I would like to know more about?
- What are some of the things I would like the writer to explain?

KEEPING IN SHAPE

Here are some other ways to get ready for writing the TAAS narrative composition.

1. Make a list of interesting words that you can substitute for the following words:

   WALKED ____________________

   ____

   ____

   ____

   SAID ____________________

   ____

   ____

   ____

   SAW ____________________

   ____

   ____

   ____

2. Here are some possible openings for stories. For each one, either draw a picture of what you think will happen next or tell a classmate.

   - Christine slammed down the phone. "She's not my friend anymore," she said . . .
   - "I never expected anything like this," said Mike as he opened his birthday present from his brother . . .
   - It was a dark and stormy night. We all sat around the campfire, telling stories, when all of a sudden . . .

3. Do you have any ideas for interesting stories of your own? Write one and share it with your classmates.

LESSON B3 THE HOW-TO COMPOSITION

This section will help you write a how-to composition by—

- showing you how to revise a low-level composition
- guiding you through the writing of your own composition
- suggesting additional ways to prepare for writing how-to compositions

THE HOW-TO COMPOSITION

Here is a prompt that asks you to write a how-to composition:

> Write a composition in which you explain to a first-grader how you clean your teeth. Tell what you use to do this job well. Describe what you do first. Then tell the other steps to take.

Here is the composition one student wrote.

> First get everything together. Especially your toothpaste and toothbrush. You take your brush and your toothpaste and put some toothpaste on. Then start brushing don't brush your gums too hard.
>
> When your done, use mouthwash. Spit it out carefully so you don't get it on your shirt.

This composition did not receive a passing score. Can you tell why? Look at "What Test Graders Look For" in the Section Guide. Then write one reason that you think this composition did not pass:

____

____

IMPROVING THE COMPOSITION

Here are some questions good writers ask themselves when they revise a composition like this one. In the blanks following each question, write the changes you would make in this composition.

1. Can my reader tell what this composition is about from the way it begins? If not, how can I change it?

____

____

2. In a how-to composition, I should tell my reader what I need to do the job. Have I done this? If not, what do I need to add?

____

____

3. In a how-to composition, I need to give all the steps for getting the job done. Have I done this? If not, what do I need to add?

____

____

4. I also need to be specific about how to do this job. (For example, what does "too hard" mean? How do you know when you have brushed "enough"?) What do I need to add so that my reader will know how to do each step of this job?

___

___

5. In a how-to composition, it's very important to have all the steps in the right order. Have I done this? What words can I add to make the order clear? Where should I add them?

___

___

6. Can my reader tell that I have finished from the way this composition ends? If not, what should I add or change?

___

___

7. Have I written complete sentences? Have I avoided fragments and run-ons? If not, what should I change? How should I change it?

___

___

8. Have I used the correct form of all pronouns, verbs, adjectives, and adverbs? If not, what changes should I make?

___

___

WRITING YOUR OWN COMPOSITION

Here is a new prompt that asks you to write a how-to composition:

> Think of something to eat that you like to make. It could be a sandwich, a dessert, a snack, a salad. Write a composition in which you tell your classmates how to make this dish. Be sure to include the things you need, and be sure to give the steps in order.

Read the prompt again, and answer these questions.

1. What things do I know how to make best?

____

____

2. What things can I explain easily and in detail to someone else?

____

____

3. Which thing am I going to write about?

____

____

4. What materials do I need? To help you answer this question, close your eyes and see yourself doing this job.

____

____

5. What steps do I take to do this job? Close your eyes and see yourself doing the job again. This time, see the complete job, from first step to last.

   Step 1

   ____

   Step 2

   ____

   Step 3

   ____

   Other Steps

   ____

   Final Step

   ____

6. What can I say at the beginning of my composition to tell my reader what I am writing about?

   ____

   ____

7. What can I say at the end to show my reader that this composition is complete?

   ____

   ____

When you have answered these questions, you have done the prewriting and planning for your composition. On the next page, there is another way to plan what you are going to write.

- Make a chart like this one and use it to help you write.
- On a separate sheet of paper, write the composition you have just planned.

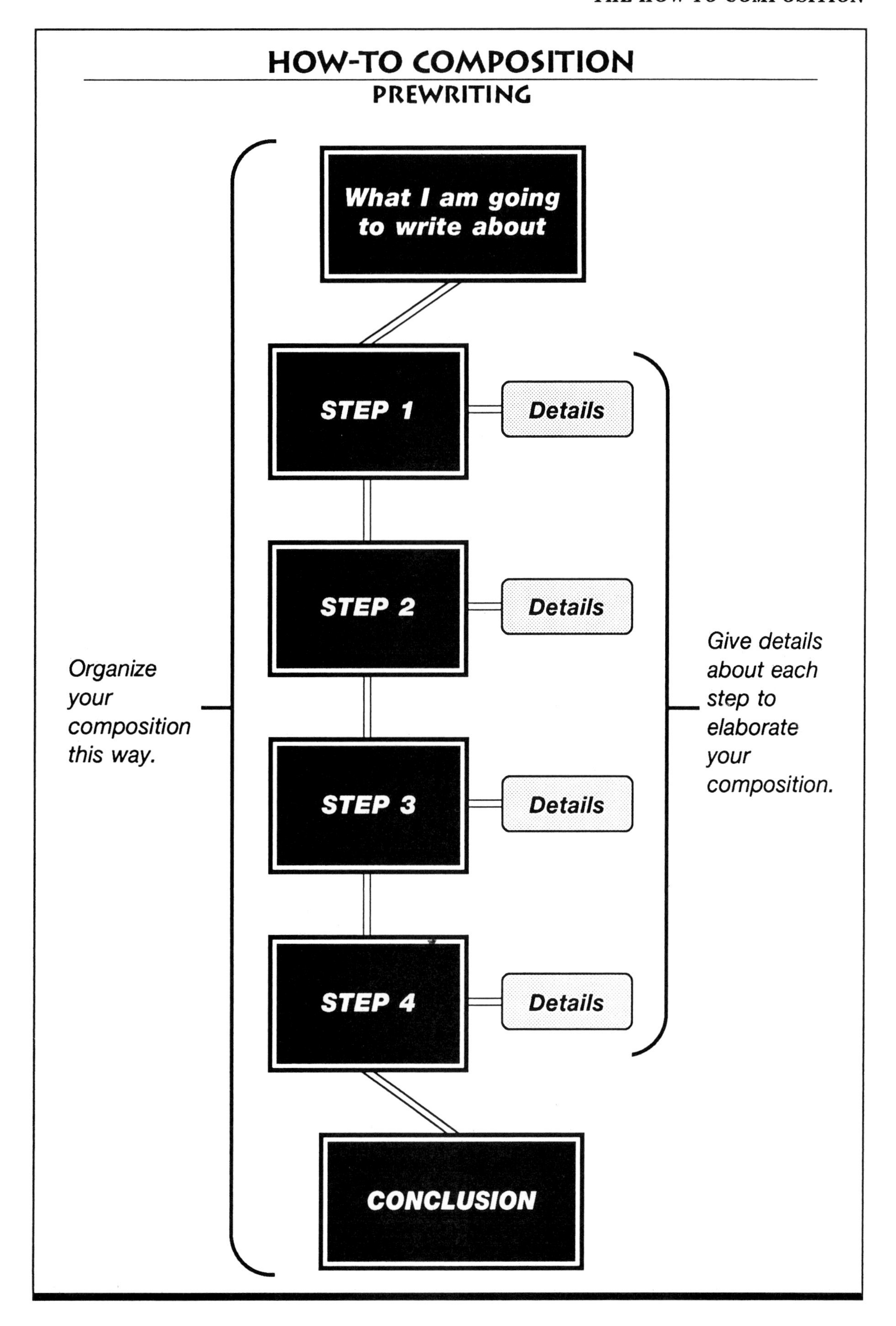
HOW-TO COMPOSITION
PREWRITING
What I am going to write about
STEP 1
Details
STEP 2
Details
STEP 3
Details
STEP 4
Details
CONCLUSION
Organize your composition this way.
Give details about each step to elaborate your composition.

AFTER YOU WRITE

Exchange papers with a classmate or share what you have written with a small group of students. Ask yourself these questions when you read or listen to your classmates' compositions:

- What are some of the things I like in this composition?
- What are some of the things I would like to know more about?
- What are some of the things I would like the writer to explain?

KEEPING IN SHAPE

Here are some other ways to get ready for writing the TAAS how-to composition.

1. Make a list of things you know how to do well.
2. Visualize yourself doing some of the things on your list. Make sure to include any materials you need and to see the steps in order.
3. Tell a classmate how to do something. Use the visualization to help you.

LESSON B4 WRITING ABOUT GOOD POINTS & BAD POINTS

This section will help you write a composition about the good and bad points of something by—

- showing you how to revise a low-level composition
- guiding you through the development of your own composition
- suggesting additional ways to prepare for writing a composition that examines good and bad points

WRITING ABOUT GOOD POINTS & BAD POINTS

Here is a prompt that asks you to write about the good points and bad points of something.

> There are both good things and bad things about doing your homework as soon as you get home from school. Write a letter to your mother or father in which you explain both what is good and what is bad about doing your homework right away.

Here is the composition one student wrote:

> Dear Mom,
>
> I am going to tell you some good things and bad things about doing homework. Homework is really boring. Why do we have to do it?
>
> If you do homework as soon as you get home, you can watch your favorite night-time TV shows. It's easier to do right after school because you just got home and you're still thinking about school. Also, you probably won't be so tired. And you'll be more rested the next day because you can get to bed earlier.

One of the bad things about doing your homework later is that you might miss things you want to watch on TV. Also, you might forget to do it. Or you might get tired and fall asleep while you're doing it and not finish it and then you would get a bad grade the next day.

So that is what I think about what is good and what is bad. What do you think?

Your daughter,

Terrie

This composition did not receive a passing score. Can you tell why? Look at "What Test Graders Look For" in the Section Guide. Then write one reason that you think this composition did not pass.

____

____

IMPROVING THE COMPOSITION

Here are some questions good writers ask themselves when they revise a composition like this one. In the blanks following each question, write the changes you would make in this composition.

1. This is a complicated prompt. Do I know what this prompt is asking me to do? Does my first paragraph show that I understand the prompt? If not, what changes should I make?

____

____

2. The reader needs to understand everything I say. Do I need to add any examples or explanations to paragraph 2? Do I need to add an example to sentence 2 of the paragraph? Do I need to explain what I mean in sentence 3? Is sentence 4 clear? What changes should I make? Write your changes on the lines at the top of the next page.

3. The prompt says to talk about the good points and bad points of doing homework right after school. Paragraph 2 talks about the good points of doing homework early. Does paragraph 3 talk about the bad things of doing homework early? If not, how do I need to change this paragraph?

4. Paragraph 3 needs to stick to the topic. What would be a good first sentence?

5. I need more than one example to make the point when I rewrite paragraph 3. What other examples or explanations can I give in this paragraph?

6. A good closing is related to the topic. It also says something that has not been said before in the composition. Does my final paragraph do these things? If not, how should I change it?

7. A good composition avoids long, rambling sentences. How would I rewrite the one in paragraph 3?

____

____

WRITING YOUR OWN COMPOSITION

Here is a new prompt that asks you to write a composition that examines good points and bad points.

> There are both good things and bad things about television. Write a composition for your teacher in which you explain both what is good and what is bad about having television.

Read the prompt again and answer these questions:

1. What subject is my composition going to be about? (*HINT:* What follows the word "about" in the prompt?)

____

____

2. What good things can I think of about television?

- _______________
- _______________
- _______________

Other things:

____

____

3. What examples or explanations can I add to each of the things I listed above?

____

____

____

4. What bad things can I think of about television?

 - ______________________________
 - ______________________________
 - ______________________________

 Other things:

____

____

5. What examples or explanations can I add to each of the things I listed above?

____

____

____

6. What can I say at the beginning of my composition to tell my reader what I am writing about?

____

____

7. What can I say at the end of my composition that is related to the topic and does not repeat something I have already said?

____

____

When you have answered these questions, you have done the prewriting and planning for your composition. On the next page there is another way to plan what you are going to write.

- Make a chart like this one and use it to help you write.
- On a separate sheet of paper, write the composition you have just planned.

GOOD POINTS & BAD POINTS COMPOSITION

PREWRITING

TOPIC

____

____

GOOD POINTS	BAD POINTS
1. ______________	1. ______________
Example or Explanation ______________	Example or Explanation ______________
______________	______________
2. ______________	2. ______________
Example or Explanation ______________	Example or Explanation ______________
______________	______________
3. ______________	3. ______________
Example or Explanation ______________	Example or Explanation ______________
______________	______________
4. ______________	4. ______________
Example or Explanation ______________	Example or Explanation ______________
______________	______________

AFTER YOU WRITE

Exchange papers with a classmate or share what you have written with a small group of students. Ask yourself these questions when you read or listen to your classmates' compositions:

- What are some of the things I like in this composition?
- What are some of the things I would like to know more about?
- What are some of the things I would like the writer to explain?

KEEPING IN SHAPE

Here are some other ways to get ready for writing the TAAS composition that examines good and bad points.

1. Think of hobbies, games, and activities that you like. For each one, make a list of both its bad points and its good points. Share your list with your classmates. See if you get any new ideas.
2. Think of things you don't like to do—for example, cleaning up your room. For each one, make a list of both its good points and its bad points. Share your list with your classmates. See if you get any new ideas.

LESSON B5 THE PERSUASIVE COMPOSITION

This section will help you write a persuasive composition by

- showing you how to revise a low-level composition
- guiding you through the writing of your own composition
- suggesting additional ways to prepare for writing a persuasive composition

THE PERSUASIVE COMPOSITION

Here is a prompt that asks you to write a persuasive composition.

> Some people like living in the city. Others like living in the country. Which do you prefer? Write a composition for your teacher, telling whether you would rather live in the city or the country. Give reasons for your choice.

Here is the composition one student wrote:

> The city and the country are both nice places. There are lots of things to do in the city. And the country is very peaceful and has animals. If I lived in the country, I could have an animal of my own. I like dogs and cats. I also like horses and pigs and cows. Wild animals are fun too.
>
> When I visit my grandparents, I like to get up in the morning to help with chores. I know how to feed the chickens and give the horses their water. I don't need an alarm clock. The roosters wake me up.

It's cheaper to live in the country you don't have to buy so much food. It's real fun. And it's good for you to live in the country.

Now you know why I think the country is better than the city.

This composition did not receive a passing score. Can you tell why? Look at "What Test Graders Look For" in the Section Guide. Then write one reason that you think this composition did not pass.

____

____

IMPROVING THE COMPOSITION

Here are some questions good writers ask themselves when they revise a composition like this one. In the blanks following each question, write the changes you would make in this composition.

1. Do I know what this prompt is asking me to do? Does my first paragraph show which choice I have made? If not, what changes should I make?

____

____

2. After I state my choice, I need to support it with reasons, facts, and examples. Have I done this in paragraph 1? Which sentences do <u>not</u> belong in this paragraph? What could I put in place of these sentences?

____

____

____

____

3. Paragraph 2 gives examples of things I like about living in the country. Do these examples illustrate one particular reason? Have I stated this reason? If not, what do I need to add?

____

____

4. I begin paragraph 3 with the reason "it's cheaper to live in the country." Have I explained this reason? Have I backed it up with enough facts or examples? What changes should I make?

____

____

5. In paragraph 3, I've given two other reasons for my choice. What facts or examples can I add to back up these reasons? Can I tell about something that has happened to me?

____

____

____

____

6. A good closing adds something new. Has my last sentence done this? If not, can I use one of the reasons I developed in step 5 above as my closing? (*HINT:* Make this reason the last paragraph of the composition. Begin the paragraph with a word like finally.)

____

____

____

____

7. Have I written complete sentences? Have I avoided fragments and run-ons? If not, what changes should I make?

____

____

WRITING YOUR OWN COMPOSITION

Here is a new prompt that asks you to write a persuasive composition.

> You have just won $35 in a safety-poster contest. Your brother thinks you should buy a new video game cartridge. Your parents want you to save the money. What do you want to do with it? Write a letter to your family, stating what you plan to do with the $35. Give reasons for your choice.

Read the prompt again and answer these questions:

1. Who am I writing to? What is my letter supposed to be about?

____

____

2. Do I like the suggestions my parents and my brother have made? If so, what do I like about these suggestions?

____

____

If not, why don't I like these suggestions?

____

____

3. What would I like to do with this money?

____

____

4. What reasons can I give for the choice I have made?
   - ___
   - ___
   - ___

5. What facts or examples can I give to elaborate my reasons? What personal experiences I can tell about that will make my reasons convincing to my family?

___

___

___

___

6. What can I say at the end of my letter that is interesting and does not repeat something I have already said?

___

___

When you have answered these questions, you have done the prewriting and planning for your composition. On the opposite page there is another way to plan what you are going to write.

- Make a chart like this one and use it to help you write.
- On a separate sheet of paper, write the composition you have just planned.

PERSUASIVE COMPOSITION

PREWRITING

OPENING

____

____

____

YOUR CHOICE

____

____

REASON 1	**REASON 2**	**REASON 3**
____________	____________	____________
____________	____________	____________
____________	____________	____________
Facts & Examples	**Facts & Examples**	**Facts & Examples**
1. ____________	1. ____________	1. ____________
2. ____________	2. ____________	2. ____________
3. ____________	3. ____________	3. ____________

CONCLUSION

____

____

____

AFTER YOU WRITE

Exchange papers with a classmate or share what you have written with a small group of students. Ask yourself these questions when you read or listen to your classmates' compositions:

- What are some of the things I like in this composition?
- What are some of the things I would like to know more about?
- What are some of the things I would like the writer to explain?

KEEPING IN SHAPE

Here are some other ways to get ready for writing the TAAS persuasive composition.

1. Think about the choices you make every day in school or at home. Make a list of these choices and think about why you made each choice. Write some of the reasons for the choices you make.

2. Think about a rule you would like to change at school or at home. Make a list of reasons for changing this rule. Make sure your reasons would convince either the principal or your family. Support your choice with facts or examples.

SECTION C
WRITING, PART 2
MULTIPLE-CHOICE QUESTIONS

C: WRITING (MULTIPLE-CHOICE QUESTIONS) SECTION GUIDE **TO THE TEACHER**

This part of *The TAAS Coach* covers the three Writing test objectives that are tested by multiple choice questions: Sentence Construction, Usage, and Mechanics (spelling, capitalization, and punctuation). It is organized the same way as the Reading section, follows the same teaching format, and can be administered the same way:

1. ***Pretest***
2. ***How to Answer TAAS Questions***
3. ***Practice with Tips***
4. ***Practice on Your Own***
5. ***Post-test***

In addition to these parts, there is a sixth part at the end of the book, which summarizes the rules that the student is expected to know for the multiple-choice Writing portion of the test:

6. ***Writer's Handbook***

The ***Pretest*** is a complete sample TAAS multiple choice Writing test. It contains 3 passages followed by 3 or 4 questions each. It is used to acquaint students with the test format and to assess their ability to handle individual targets. Further practice can be individualized based on the results of the pretest.

How to Answer TAAS Questions reviews the questions of the Pretest. This section models the type of thinking that students need to pursue when answering TAAS questions. It examines each question in order, using "Think Along" models to help students develop strategies for answering each type of question.

This section may be used individually, in small groups, or in whole-class settings. Where time permits, students may go through all the lessons in this section.

For speed, each student can be assigned work on only those lessons that review Pretest questions that he or she missed.

The lessons in "How to Answer TAAS Questions" should be used in combination with the ***Writer's Handbook.*** Each lesson contains, under the heading "RESEARCH," a cross reference to the section of the Writer's Handbook that covers the TAAS instructional target that is being tested. You may wish to have students consult the Handbook before working through the Think-Along portion of the lesson.

You may also wish to assign sections of the Handbook as in-class work or as homework.

Practice with Tips is a second complete sample test, consisting of three new Writing test passages plus questions. This section gives students guided practice in answering TAAS questions. Helpful hints printed in the margin next to each question remind the student of the important strategies learned in the previous section on How to Answer TAAS Questions.

Practice on Your Own is a third complete sample test with questions. This section gives students independent practice on taking the exam. No hints are given on how to answer the questions.

The ***Post-test*** is a final check of students' mastery of the test objectives and format.

C: WRITING (MULTIPLE-CHOICE QUESTIONS) SECTION GUIDE TO THE STUDENT

The second part of the TAAS Writing exam is a multiple-choice test like the reading test. It tests all of the following things:

1. ***Sentence construction.*** Can you spot incomplete sentences, run-on sentences, or sentences that need to be combined? Do you know how to correct all these mistakes in sentence construction?

2. ***Usage.*** Can you supply the correct form of a word in a sentence?

3. ***Spelling, capitalization, and punctuation.*** Can you spot mistakes in all three of these areas? Can you correct the mistakes you spot?

This section of *The TAAS Coach* will show you how to answer the kinds of questions you will meet on the test.

To do well on this section of the TAAS Writing test, you have to know some facts and rules about writing correctly. The section called *Writer's Handbook* at the end section of the book will show you all the facts and rules you need to know.

It also helps to know a few tips that will help you be a better test taker. Read the ones below carefully. Try to remember them and use them.

TIPS ON CHOOSING THE RIGHT ANSWER

Remember that only one answer is correct. All the information you need to answer the question is in the passage.

Here are some important tips.

1. ***Read all the choices.*** You may be sure you've found the correct answer choice. But don't mark your answer sheet until you have looked at the other choices.

If they're wrong, you should know the reasons why. You should also have a good reason for choosing the correct answer.

2. ***Write in your booklet.*** You can underline ideas or make notes in the margin. Notes can help you find important ideas again quickly.

3. ***Answer all the questions.*** A good guess is better than nothing.

4. ***Eliminate wrong answers.*** If you don't know the right answer, find the ones you think are wrong. The one that's left is probably right.

Sample Passage A

Read the passage. Some sections are underlined. The underlined sections may be one of the following:

- **Incomplete sentences**
- **Run-ons**
- **Correctly written sentences that should be combined**
- **Correctly written sentences that do not need to be rewritten**

Choose the best way to write each underlined section. If the underlined section needs no change, mark "D No Mistake."

Learning to juggle takes time. But a lot of fun. (1) Most jugglers begin juggling with small balls or bean bags. First they practice throwing one ball from the left hand to the right hand then they throw two. (2) Finally they have all three balls going at once.

Later they can learn to juggle clubs. They can learn to juggle plates. They can even learn to juggle knives. (3)

1. **A** Because it is a lot of fun, learning to juggle takes time.
   B Learning to juggle takes time, but it is a lot of fun.
   C Learning to juggle takes time. But what a lot of fun!
   D No mistake.

2. **A** First they practice throwing one ball. From the left hand to the right hand. Then they throw two.
   B After they throw one ball from the left hand to the right hand. Then they throw two.
   C First they practice throwing one ball from the left hand to the right hand. Then they throw two.
   D No mistake

3. **A** Later they can learn to juggle clubs, or they can also learn how to juggle plates, or they can even learn how to juggle knives as well.
   B Later they can learn to juggle clubs, they can juggle plates or even knives.
   C Later they can learn to juggle clubs, plates, or even knives.
   D No mistake

Sample Passage B

Read the passage and choose the word or group of words that belongs in each space. Mark the letter for your answer.

Our class had to make a graph of the kinds of cars in a parking lot. ___(1)___ decided to make a picture graph. After school we ___(2)___ to the supermarket parking lot to find out what makes of cars people used. First we counted all the American cars. Then we counted the cars that came from Europe and from Japan. We saved the ___(3)___ part for last—drawing the graph. None of us is a real artist, so we always ___(4)___ slowly and carefully when we do projects like this one. When we finished, we thought the graph looked pretty good.

1 **A** Me and Antonio
B Antonio and I
C Antonio and myself
D Myself and Antonio

2 **A** go
B goed
C went
D gone

3 **A** hardest
B most hardest
C harder
D more harder

4 **A** works
B work
C is working
D was working

Sample Passage C

Read the passage and decide which type of mistake, if any, appears in each underlined section. Mark the letter for your answer.

Nowadays swimmers and hikers love the lakes rivers and pine forests (1) of the Adirondack Mountains in upstate New York. a hundred years ago there (2) were factories in these mountains. One factory near Lake George used the local pine (3) to make wooden pencils. Graphite was dug from nearby mines to fill the pencils. Later the mine workers started a town near the mines. What do you think they named it? It's not hard to make the right gess. (4) The town was named Graphite.

1 **A** Spelling
B Capitalization
C Punctuation
D No Mistake

2 **A** Spelling
B Capitalization
C Punctuation
D No Mistake

3 **A** Spelling
B Capitalization
C Punctuation
D No Mistake

4 **A** Spelling
B Capitalization
C Punctuation
D No Mistake

LESSON C1
ANSWERING SENTENCE CONSTRUCTION QUESTIONS

OBJECTIVE: Recognize appropriate sentence construction within the context of a written passage.

HOW TO ANSWER THE QUESTIONS
PRETEST SAMPLE PASSAGE A

Here's how to answer questions like the ones that follow Sample Passage A of the Writing Pretest.

1. Look at the underlined part of the passage. Ask yourself if it has any of these mistakes:

   - It's an incomplete sentence (sometimes called "a fragment").
   - It's a run-on sentence.
   - It is made of sentences that need to be combined.

2. If you spot any of these mistakes, look at the first 3 answer choices. Pick the one that corrects the mistake.

   Be sure that your answer choice means the same thing as the original!

   Your answer should follow the rules for incomplete sentences, run-ons, and putting sentences together. They are in the "Sentence Combination" section of *The Writer's Handbook* at the end of the book.

3. If you don't find any mistake, choose "D No mistake" as your answer.

QUESTION 1

TARGET: *Recognize complete sentences and avoid fragments and run-ons*

<u>Learning to juggle takes time. But a lot of fun.</u>
(1)

1 **A** Because it is a lot of fun, learning to juggle takes time.
B Learning to juggle takes time, but it is a lot of fun.
C Learning to juggle takes time. But what a lot of fun!
D No mistake

RESEARCH

The section in the *Writer's Handbook* that covers this question is called **SENTENCE CONSTRUCTION: 1. Incomplete Sentences.** You may want to read it before you go any further.

THINK-ALONG

This is the way you should think when you answer the question.

Read this part slowly and carefully. Your teacher may also read it aloud to you. Look at the answer choices and the passage when you need to.

First I'll see if there's anything wrong with the underlined sentences.

The first sentence looks OK. But the second sentence is incomplete. That's the problem, right there.

Now let me look at the answer choices.

- A is a good sentence. The incomplete sentence is attached to the first sentence. But wait—the new sentence means something different. And it doesn't make sense. Learning to juggle takes time because it's hard, not because it's fun.
- B looks better. The incomplete sentence is attached to the first sentence. The new sentence means the same thing as the two original ones. But I'll check the other answers anyway.
- C still contains a fragment—"But what a lot of fun!" So it's wrong.
- D says "No mistake." But I already know that there is a mistake—the incomplete sentence.

The correct answer is B.

REMEMBER

A group of words that begins with a capital letter and ends with a period might not always be a sentence.

QUESTION 2

TARGET: *Recognize complete sentences and avoid fragments and run-ons*

First they practice throwing one ball from the
(2)
left hand to the right hand then they throw two.

2 **A** First they practice throwing one ball. From the left hand to the right hand. Then they throw two.

B After they throw one ball from the left hand to the right hand. Then they throw two.

C First they practice throwing one ball from the left hand to the right hand. Then they throw two.

D No mistake

RESEARCH

The section in the *Writer's Handbook* that covers this question is called **SENTENCE CONSTRUCTION: 2. Run-on Sentences.** You may want to read it before you go any further.

THINK-ALONG

This is the way you should think when you answer the question.

Read this part slowly and carefully. Your teacher may also read it aloud to you. Look at the answer choices and the passage when you need to.

First I'll see if there's anything wrong with the underlined sentence.

It's not an incomplete sentence. But it is a run-on. That's what's wrong.

Let me look at the answer choices. I'll pick the one that fixes the problem.

- A seems to fix the run-on. But that second sentence is wrong. It's an incomplete sentence! This answer choice is incorrect. It fixes one mistake and puts in another.
- B is even worse. The first sentence is incomplete. And there's nothing about "after" in the original.
- C looks good. The run-on is broken up into two good sentences. This must be correct.
- D is wrong, since there is a mistake.

REMEMBER

Look closely at a long sentence that has no punctuation in the middle or just a comma in the middle. It might really be two sentences.

QUESTION 3

TARGET: *Combine sentence parts and sentences to produce a variety of sentence structures.*

> Later they can learn to juggle clubs. They can learn
> (3)
> to juggle plates. They can even learn to juggle knives.

3 **A** Later they can learn to juggle clubs, or they can also learn how to juggle plates, or they can even learn how to juggle knives as well.

B Later they can learn to juggle clubs, they can juggle plates or even knives.

C Later they can learn to juggle clubs, plates, or even knives.

D No mistake

RESEARCH

The section in the *Writer's Handbook* that covers this question is called **SENTENCE CONSTRUCTION: 3. Combining Sentences.** You may want to read it before you go any further.

THINK-ALONG

This is the way you should think when you answer the question.

Read this part slowly and carefully. Your teacher may also read it aloud to you. Look at the answer choices and the passage when you need to.

The underlined sentences look OK. There are no incomplete sentences or run-ons. But they repeat words a lot. They probably should be combined.

Let me check the answer choices.

- A combines the sentences, but it doesn't take out any words. It even adds extra words. It's not an improvement. This choice is wrong.
- B combines the sentences, but it turns them into a run-on. So this choice is wrong, too.
- C combines the sentences and drops unnecessary words. The new sentence is not a run-on. So I guess this answer choice is correct.
- D can't be right, since C is an improvement over the sentences in the passage.

C is the correct answer.

REMEMBER

Combine short sentences that have repeated words to make them more interesting.

LESSON C2
ANSWERING USAGE QUESTIONS

OBJECTIVE: Recognize appropriate English usage within the context of a written paragraph.

HOW TO ANSWER THE QUESTIONS

PRETEST SAMPLE PASSAGE B

Here's how to answer questions like the ones that follow Sample Writing Passage B of the Writing Pretest.

1. Put each of the answer choices in the blank.

2. Whisper the whole sentence to yourself. Listen to how each answer choice sounds. Does one sound better than the other?

3. Your answer should follow the rules for the forms of pronouns, verbs, adjectives, and adverbs. They are in the "Usage" section of *The Writer's Handbook* at the end of the book. Which answer choice fits the rules?

QUESTION 1

***TARGET**: Use the correct subject, object, and possessive forms of pronouns.*

> ___(1)___ decided to make a picture graph.

1 **A** Me and Antonio
B Antonio and I
C Antonio and myself
D Myself and Antonio

RESEARCH

The section in the *Writer's Handbook* that covers this question is called **USAGE: 1. Pronoun Forms.** You may want to read it before you go any further.

THINK-ALONG

This is the way you should think when you answer the question.

Read this part slowly and carefully. Your teacher may also read it aloud to you. Look at the answer choices and the passage when you need to.

I'll try each answer choice in the blank.

- A is "Me and Antonio decided to make a picture graph." OK. Let me try it with the pronoun alone: "Me decided to make a picture graph." That sounds awful.
- B is "Antonio and I decided to make a picture graph." That sounds OK. You need a subject form in the blank space, and the only correct subject form of the pronoun is "I." That's what the Handbook says, in the section about pronoun forms.

  (An important clue is that the blank is at the beginning of the sentence, where the subject is usually found.)
- C and D aren't right. I know that myself is not the subject form of the pronoun. It sounds bad to say "Myself decided to make a picture graph for Ms. Jackson's class."

I'll choose B.

REMEMBER

To make sure you have the right form of the pronoun, take away the noun and the word and. Say the sentence with just the pronoun.

QUESTION 2

TARGET: *Recognize correct verb tense and correct form of tense of irregular verbs.*

After school we __(2)__ to the supermarket parking lot to find out what makes of cars people used.

2 **A** go
B goed
C went
D gone

RESEARCH

The section in the *Writer's Handbook* that covers this question is called **USAGE: 3. Verb Tenses and the Forms of Irregular Verbs.** You may want to read this section before you go any further. Be sure to look at the chart of irregular verb forms.

THINK-ALONG

This is the way you should think when you answer the question.

Read this part slowly and carefully. Your teacher may also read it aloud to you. Look at the answer choices and the passage when you need to.

As usual, I'll put each answer choice in the blank and see if it belongs.

- A is "After school we go to the supermarket parking lot." That's wrong. The action of the story is in the past. *Go* is a present tense form. It should be a past tense form.
- B is "After school we goed to the supermarket parking lot." That's not right. *Go* is an irregular verb. Its past tense doesn't end in *-ed.* You don't say *we goed*. You say *we went.*
- C is "After school we went to the supermarket parking lot." That's what I just said. That's correct. You need a past tense of the verb *go* in the blank space, and the correct past tense is *went.* But I'll check D just in case.
- D is "After school we *gone* to the supermarket parking lot." No, that's wrong. You could say *have gone,* but not *gone* by itself.

C is correct.

REMEMBER

When the action of a passage begins in the past tense, look for answer choices in the past tense.

Also, know the list of irregular verbs forms listed in the *Writer's Handbook* at the end of this book. This list shows you the correct forms to use in speech and writing.

QUESTION 3

TARGET: *Use the correct forms of adjectives and adverbs.*

> First we counted all the American cars. Then we counted the cars that came from Europe and from Japan. We saved the __(3)__ part for last—drawing the graph.

3 **A** hardest
B most hardest
C harder
D more harder

RESEARCH

The section in the *Writer's Handbook* that covers this question is called **USAGE: 4. Forms of Adjectives and Adverbs.** You may want to read it before you go any further.

THINK-ALONG

This is the way you should think when you answer the question.

Read this part slowly and carefully. Your teacher may also read it aloud to you. Look at the answer choices and the passage when you need to.

- A is "We saved the hardest part for last." Well, the project has lots of steps. So I guess you'd say *hardest*, not *harder*. This may be the correct form right here. But let me check the rest of the answer choices.
- B is "We saved the most hardest part for last." I know that's wrong. You can't put *most* in front of a form that ends in *-er* or *-est*.
- C and D are both wrong. You don't use the form *harder* unless you're comparing only two things. And the form *more harder* is always wrong.

B is the correct choice.

REMEMBER

Add -er or more to an adjective or adverb when you are comparing two things. DO NOT ADD BOTH.

Add -est or most to an adjective or adverb when you are comparing more than two things. DO NOT ADD BOTH.

QUESTION 4

TARGET: *Use correct subject-verb agreement with personal pronouns and compound subjects..*

None of us is a real artist, so we always ___(4)___ slowly and carefully when we do projects like this one. When we finished, we thought the graph looked pretty good.

4 **A** works
B work
C is working
D was working

RESEARCH

The sections in the *Writer's Handbook* that cover this question are called **USAGE: 2. Subject-Verb Agreement** and the first part of **3. Verb Tenses and the Forms of Irregular Verbs.** You may want to read these sections before you go any further.

THINK-ALONG

This is the way you should think when you answer the question.

Read this part slowly and carefully. Your teacher may also read it aloud to you. Look at the answer choices and the passage when you need to.

- A is "We always works slowly." This is wrong because the pronoun *we* always goes with a plural form of a verb in the present tense. The plural form doesn't have -*s* or -*es* at the end.
- B is "We always work slowly." This looks correct. It is the correct verb form to go with the pronoun *we*. But I'll check C and D just to be careful.
- C and D are incorrect because both *is* and *was* are forms that go with the pronouns *he, she,* and *it.* They don't go with *we*.

So B is still the best choice.

REMEMBER

The present tense of a verb ends in -s or -es. Use this form with the pronouns he, she, it. Practice by saying the verbs in the following way.

I work.	**We** work.
You work.	**You** work.
He, **she**, or **it** works.	**They** work.

LESSON C3 SPELLING, CAPITALIZATION, & PUNCTUATION

OBJECTIVE: Recognize appropriate spelling, capitalization, and punctuation within the context of a written paragraph.

HOW TO ANSWER THE QUESTIONS

PRETEST SAMPLE PASSAGE C

Here's how to answer questions like the ones that follow Sample Writing Passage C of the Writing Pretest.

1. Look at each set of underlined words. Ask yourself three questions:

   - Is all the ***spelling*** correct?
   - Is the ***capitalization*** correct?
   - Is the ***punctuation*** correct?

   Ask these questions one at a time! You can't check for all three things at once.

2. If you find a mistake, it will be in only one of the three areas. That's the answer choice you should pick.

3. If there's no mistake, choose "D No mistake."

Remember, you don't have to correct the error. You just have to find it and identify what kind it is.

QUESTION 1

TARGET: *Use the fundamentals of spelling, capitalization, and punctuation.*

> Nowadays swimmers and hikers love the
> (1)
> lakes rivers and pine forests of the Adirondack
>
> Mountains . . .

1 **A** Spelling
B Capitalization
C Punctuation
D No Mistake

RESEARCH

The section in the *Writer's Handbook* that covers this question is called **PUNCTUATION: 2. Commas.** You may want to read it before you go any further.

THINK-ALONG

This is the way you should think when you answer the question.

Read this part slowly and carefully. Your teacher may also read it aloud to you. Look at the answer choices and the passage when you need to.

- A is Spelling. It looks OK to me. I don't see anything misspelled.
- B is Capitalization. It looks OK. None of the underlined words needs to be capitalized.
- C is Punctuation. The words aren't at the end of a sentence, and there aren't any abbreviations, so I don't have to look for a period.

  What about commas? Ah, there's the mistake. You're supposed to put commas between three or more words in a series. The sentence should be punctuated like this:

  > Nowadays swimmers and hikers love the lakes**,** rivers**,** and pine forests of the Adirondack Mountains . . .

- D "No mistake" is incorrect. There is a mistake.

C is the correct answer.

REMEMBER

Commas are used to separate words in a series. When you see a string of words in a series, check for commas.

QUESTION 2

TARGET: *Use the fundamentals of spelling, capitalization, and punctuation.*

> Nowadays swimmers and hikers love the lakes rivers and pine forests of the Adirondack Mountains in upstate New York. a hundred years ago there (2) were factories in these mountains.

2 **A** Spelling
B Capitalization
C Punctuation
D No Mistake

RESEARCH

The section in the *Writer's Handbook* that covers this question is called **CAPITALIZATION.** You may want to read it before you go any further.

THINK-ALONG

This is the way you should think when you answer the question.

Read this part slowly and carefully. Your teacher may also read it aloud to you. Look at the answer choices and the passage when you need to.

- A is Spelling. It looks OK, but I'm not sure about the word *there*. I think it's correctly spelled, but it might be *their*. I don't know about this choice yet. But I'll go on.
- B is Capitalization. Well, there's the mistake right there. The sentence that starts a hundred years ago should have the first word capitalized: ***A** hundred years ago there were factories in the mountains.* So *there* is the correct spelling after all.
- C is Punctuation, but it looks OK to me. Anyhow, I know the problem is the missing capital letter at the beginning of the sentence.
- D is wrong, since there's a missing capital letter.

B is the correct answer.

REMEMBER

Always begin a sentence with a capital letter. When you are taking the TAAS test, take a good look at the word that follows the end of a sentence. If there is no capital letter, you can be sure that there is a punctuation error.

QUESTION 3

TARGET: *Use the fundamentals of spelling, capitalization, and punctuation.*

One factory near Lake George used the local
(3)
pine to make wooden pencils.

3 **A** Spelling
B Capitalization
C Punctuation
D No Mistake

RESEARCH

You don't need to do any research for this question. After you read the Think-Along, you'll know why.

THINK-ALONG

This is the way you should think when you answer the question.

Read this part slowly and carefully. Your teacher may also read it aloud to you. Look at the answer choices and the passage when you need to.

- A is Spelling. It looks OK to me. I don't see anything misspelled.
- B is Capitalization. It looks OK. The sentence begins with a capital letter. *Lake George* is the name of a place, and so it's a proper noun. It should be capitalized.
- C is Punctuation. The words aren't at the end of a sentence, and there aren't any abbreviations, so I don't have to look for a period or any other end punctuation. And I don't see any reason to put a comma in anywhere. What's the mistake in this passage, anyway?
- Wait a minute! If there isn't any mistake, then the correct answer is "D No mistake"!

I'm choosing D. I can't find any mistake in the underlined passage.

REMEMBER

Not every underlined section in a passage contains an error. Check the obvious possibilities:

- ☐ Does every sentence begin with a capital?
- ☐ Does every sentence end with the proper punctuation?
- ☐ Are all proper nouns capitalized? All book titles?
- ☐ The pronoun ***I***?
- ☐ Are all words spelled correctly?
- ☐ Are commas used to separate items in a list?
- ☐ Are apostrophes used in possessives and contractions?

QUESTION 4

TARGET: Use the fundamentals of spelling, capitalization, and punctuation.

You probably made the right gess.
(4)

4 **A** Spelling
B Capitalization
C Punctuation
D No Mistake

RESEARCH

The section in the *Writer's Handbook* that covers this question is called **SPELLING.** You may want to look it over before you go any further.

THINK-ALONG

This is the way you should think when you answer the question.

Read this part slowly and carefully. Your teacher may also read it aloud to you. Look at the answer choices and the passage when you need to.

Let me look for mistakes, one at a time.

- A is Spelling. Well, the only two hard words are *right* and *gess*. I know *right* is OK. But *gess*? That's wrong! It's supposed to be spelled G-U-E-S-S. That's the right answer choice, right there. It's a spelling mistake.
- B is an incorrect choice because there are no capitalization errors. The sentence begins with a capital letter, there is no pronoun ***I***, and there are no proper nouns.
- C is a wrong choice too. There's a period at the end of the sentence. That's the only punctuation that the sentence needs.
- D is incorrect because there is a spelling error.

A is the right answer choice.

REMEMBER

If you think a word is misspelled, write it on a piece of paper. If you have practiced writing your spelling words, your fingers will help you remember the correct spelling!

SECTION C
PRACTICE WITH TIPS

Sample Passage D

Read the passage. Some sections are underlined. The underlined sections may be one of the following:

- **Incomplete sentences**
- **Run-ons**
- **Correctly written sentences that should be combined**
- **Correctly written sentences that do not need to be rewritten**

Choose the best way to write each underlined section. If the underlined section needs no change, mark "D No mistake."

Gertrude Bonnin was a Lakota Indian. Gertrude was from a Sioux reservation. The reservation was in South Dakota. (1) She wrote about being sent away to school in Indiana. Gertrude wasn't her real name it was changed when she went to school. (2) Her Indian name was "Red Bird." Red Bird became a writer. When she grew up. (3) She described her trip to Indiana and her new life there. Everything at school was confusing and frightening. Red Bird tried to hide under the bed, but the teachers pulled her out. (4)

TIP: *Combine short sentences to make them more interesting. Do not change the meaning of the original. Avoid fragments and run-ons when you combine.*

1 A Gertrude Bonnin was a Lakota Indian. From a Sioux reservation in South Dakota.

B A Lakota Indian from South Dakota, Gertrude Bonnin grew up there, on a Sioux reservation in South Dakota.

C Gertrude Bonnin was a Lakota Indian from a Sioux reservation in South Dakota.

D Gertrude Bonnin was a Lakota Indian she was from a Sioux reservation in South Dakota.

TIP: *Look again at a long sentence with no punctuation in the middle, or with a comma in the middle. It might be two sentences.*

2 **A** Gertrude wasn't her real name. It was changed when she went to school.

B Not her real name, Gertrude was changed when she went to school.

C Gertrude wasn't her real name. It was changed. When she went to school.

D No mistake

TIP: *A group of words that begins with a capital letter and ends with a period may not be a sentence.*

3 **A** Red Bird grew up she became a writer.

B Red Bird became a writer when she grew up.

C Red Bird became a writer and she grew up.

D No mistake

TIP: *You're on your own!*

4 **A** Everything at school was confusing and frightening Red Bird tried to hide under the bed. But the teachers pulled her out.

B Everything at school was confusing and frightening Red Bird tried to hide under the bed the teachers pulled her out.

C Everything at school was confusing. Everything was frightening. Red Bird tried to hide. She tried to hide under the bed. But the teachers pulled her out.

D No mistake

Sample Passage E

Read the passage and choose the word or group of words that belongs in each space. Mark the letter for your answer.

> Eileen and I __(1)__ our new pet. It is a blue parakeet with yellow feathers on __(2)__ face. We have named our bird Fluffy. Fluffy's best trick is to kiss __(3)__ whenever we say "Pretty boy" to him. One day Fluffy __(4)__ to the mirror, said "Pretty boy," and kissed himself! It was the __(5)__ thing we had ever seen. It's easy to believe that parrots and parakeets are almost as smart as people.

TIP: *A compound subject is like a plural subject. Choose the form of the verb that agrees with it.*

1 **A** is loving
B loves
C was loving
D love

TIP: *Pronouns have special forms when they are used to show possession.*

2 **A** its
B its'
C it's
D it

TIP: *If you are not sure which form of the pronoun is correct in a compound object, try using the pronoun alone.*

3 **A** I and Eileen
B Eileen and me
C Eileen and I
D Eileen and myself

TIP: *Some verbs have special forms in the past tense.*

4 **A** flown
B flied
C flew
D flies

TIP: *Use -est or most to compare more than two things.*

5 **A** cuter
B cutest
C most cutest
D most cuter

Sample Passage F

Read the passage and decide which type of mistake, if any, appears in each underlined section. Mark the letter for your answer.

Some scientists in the <u>state of massachusetts</u> (1) have been making special robots. These robots look like insects and have funny names. <u>Three of them are named Tooth Toto and Genghis.</u> (2) The idea for these robots came from studying insects.

Their brains are sort of like <u>an insect's brain.</u> (3) They look like something <u>invented by Dr Frankenstein.</u> (4) Yet someday they might be used to explore Mars.

TIP: *Capitalize proper nouns.*

1 **A** Spelling
B Capitalization
C Punctuation
D No mistake

TIP: *Use a comma between words in a series.*

2 **A** Spelling
B Capitalization
C Punctuation
D No mistake

TIP: *Use an apostrophe in possessives.*

3 **A** Spelling
B Capitalization
C Punctuation
D No mistake

TIP: *Use a period after an abbreviation.*

4 **A** Spelling
B Capitalization
C Punctuation
D No mistake

Sample Passage G

Read the passage. Some sections are underlined. The underlined sections may be one of the following:

- **Incomplete sentences**
- **Run-ons**
- **Correctly written sentences that should be combined**
- **Correctly written sentences that do not need to be rewritten**

Choose the best way to write each underlined section. If the underlined section needs no change, mark "D—No mistake."

Wolf hybrids are dogs that are part wolf. <u>This is a good combination. Because wolves are smart, friendly animals.</u> (1) They are kind and loyal to each other. <u>Wolves live in a pack, with one adult male and one adult female who are the pack leaders.</u> (2) A wolf hybrid might decide that its human owner is the pack leader. <u>It might want the human to protect it. It might want the human to tell it what to do.</u> (3) It won't bark at strangers. <u>This animal is a very gentle and sweet pet, it is not a good watchdog.</u> (4)

1 **A** This is a good combination because wolves are smart, friendly animals.

B This is a good combination wolves are smart, friendly animals.

C Because this is a good combination, wolves are smart, friendly animals.

D No mistake

2 **A** Wolves live in a pack. With one adult male and one adult female who are the pack leaders.

B Wolves live in a pack. With one adult male and one adult female. Who are the pack leaders.

C Wolves live in a pack, with one adult male and one adult female. Who are the pack leaders.

D No mistake

3 **A** It might want the human to protect it. And tell it what to do.

B It might want the human to protect it and tell it what to do.

C It might want the human to protect it. Telling it what to do.

D No mistake

4 **A** This animal is a very gentle and sweet pet it is not a good watchdog.

B This animal is a very gentle and sweet pet. Not a good watchdog.

C This animal is a very gentle and sweet pet, but it is not a good watchdog.

D No mistake

Sample Passage H

Read the passage and choose the word or group of words that belongs in each space. Mark the letter for your answer.

Last names like García or Gonzales __(1)__ very common in Spanish. Lopez and Sanchez are also among the names that occur __(2)__. Sometimes the last name comes from a family relationship. I never __(3)__, for example, that Martinez means "Martin's son." __(4)__ name might also be the name of an occupation or a place. Long ago, the first people that had the name Ferrer __(5)__ probably blacksmiths. García is the name of a town in Spain.

1
- **A** was
- **B** is
- **C** are
- **D** am

2
- **A** more frequent
- **B** most frequent
- **C** most frequently
- **D** more frequenter

3
- **A** knew
- **B** knowed
- **C** known
- **D** knows

4
- **A** Your'
- **B** You
- **C** You're
- **D** Your

5
- **A** were
- **B** are
- **C** is
- **D** was

Sample Passage I

Read the passage and decide which type of mistake, if any, appears in each underlined section. Mark the letter for your answer.

<u>Dear Tanya</u>
(1)

You probably <u>thought i was</u> (2) never going to answer your letter. I have been very <u>busey writing a report</u> (3) for school. It was on codes and other secret languages. I found an article in the library called <u>"Navajo Code talkers."</u> (4) It told about the Navajo Marines in World War II. They used their language as a code. People from other <u>countries couldn't understand them.</u> (5) Maybe we could write in a code like that.

<u>Your cousin,</u>
(6)
Nicole

1 **A** Spelling
B Capitalization
C Punctuation
D No mistake

2 **A** Spelling
B Capitalization
C Punctuation
D No mistake

3 **A** Spelling
B Capitalization
C Punctuation
D No mistake

4 **A** Spelling
B Capitalization
C Punctuation
D No mistake

5 **A** Spelling
B Capitalization
C Punctuation
D No mistake

6 **A** Spelling
B Capitalization
C Punctuation
D No mistake

SECTION C POST-TEST

Sample Passage J

Read the passage. Some sections are underlined. The underlined sections may be one of the following:

- **Incomplete sentences**
- **Run-ons**
- **Correctly written sentences that should be combined**
- **Correctly written sentences that do not need to be rewritten**

Choose the best way to write each underlined section. If the underlined section needs no change, mark "D No mistake."

The Rio Grande is a large river. The Rio Grande forms the border between Texas and Mexico. (1) However, it is not just a Texas river. It begins in the mountains of Colorado. And flows through New Mexico. (2) The river moves slowly through Texas, but in New Mexico it runs fast. There it is wild. And free. (3) The water bubbles over rocks, forming rapids. Many people ride rafts down the rapids in the spring it is an exciting and adventurous trip. (4)

1
- **A** The Rio Grande is a large river and it also forms the border between Texas and Mexico too.
- **B** The Rio Grande is a large river that forms the border between Texas and Mexico.
- **C** Because it forms the border between Texas and Mexico, the Rio Grande is a large river
- **D** No mistake

2
- **A** In the mountains of Colorado it begins. Then through New Mexico.
- **B** It begins in New Mexico and flows through the mountains of Colorado.
- **C** It begins in the mountains of Colorado and flows through New Mexico.
- **D** No mistake

3 **A** There it is wild and free.

B There it is wild. Also it is free there.

C Wild there, it is free.

D No mistake

4 **A** Riding down the rapids in the spring, it is exciting.

B Many people ride rafts down the rapids. In the spring, when it is an exciting trip.

C Many people ride rafts down the rapids in the spring. It is an exciting and adventurous trip.

D No mistake

Sample Passage K

Read the passage and choose the word or group of words that belongs in each space.

> ___(1)___ are very interested in Texas history. We particularly ___(2)___ to read about how the cowboys herded longhorn cattle from Texas to Kansas. There were many different ways to go from San Antonio to Abilene, but the ___(3)___ way of all was known as Chisholm Trail. This trail was named after Jesse Chisholm, whose wagon wheels ___(4)___ the path from Kansas to Oklahoma. Cowboys knew they could drive the cattle ___(5)___ to the stockyards by staying on this trail.

1 **A** My brother and me
  B My brother and I
  C Myself and my brother
  D My brother and myself

2 **A** liking
  B likes
  C has like
  D like

3 **A** directest
  B most direct
  C directer
  D more direct

4 **A** wore
  B are wearing
  C has wore
  D weared

5 **A** safe
  B safer
  C most safe
  D safely

Sample Passage L

Read the passage and decide which type of mistake, if any, appears in each underlined section.

17 Sandpebble Drive

Houston Texas
(1)
October 10, 1992

Dear Ms. Jordan,
(2)

Last week in school i read (3) an article about you in a book called *the TAAS coach grade five english language arts.* (4) The article said, "she had been brought up (5) to believe that she could be anything she wanted to be." I wold like to be (6) an astronaut. What should I do to make my dream come true?

Yours truly
(7)
Graciela Archuleta

1 **A** Spelling
B Capitalization
C Punctuation
D No mistake

2 **A** Spelling
B Capitalization
C Punctuation
D No mistake

3 **A** Spelling
B Capitalization
C Punctuation
D No mistake

4 **A** Spelling
B Capitalization
C Punctuation
D No mistake

5 **A** Spelling
B Capitalization
C Punctuation
D No mistake

6 **A** Spelling
B Capitalization
C Punctuation
D No mistake

7 **A** Spelling
B Capitalization
C Punctuation
D No mistake

APPENDIX WRITER'S HANDBOOK

All the rules that you need to know for this part of the TAAS Writing test are in the following pages—*the TAAS Writer's Handbook.*

Your teacher may give you certain sections to read, discuss, and practice every day in school or for homework.

Your teacher may also suggest that you memorize certain words and rules.

SENTENCE CONSTRUCTION

TARGET: ***Recognize complete sentences and avoid fragments and run-ons.***

TARGET: ***Combine sentence parts and sentences to produce a variety of sentence structures including basic sentence patterns and variations.***

1. INCOMPLETE SENTENCES (SENTENCE FRAGMENTS)

An ***incomplete sentence***, or ***sentence fragment***, is a group of words that looks like a sentence but is not complete. It has a capital letter at the beginning and a period at the end, but part of the sentence is missing. Look at these two examples:

Because parrots can bring two toes together.

Hanging onto a branch with one foot.

Here are two ways to recognize fragments.

1. Words like ***because, before, after, although, when,*** and ***if*** are a signal to look for a two-part sentence like this one:

   Because parrots can bring two toes together,
   their feet are like human hands.

Watch out. If you see only one part of the sentence, the sentence is probably incomplete. You need to attach this fragment to another sentence.

2. Words that end in ***-ing*** or ***-ed*** can also be a signal that a sentence is incomplete. Fragments like these also need to be attached to a sentence:

   Hanging onto a branch with one foot,
   a parrot can use its other foot to eat seeds.

PRACTICE:

Underline the incomplete sentence:

1. Attached to its owner, a parrot can be very jealous of other people.
2. Parrots learn to talk easily. When they live in captivity.

2. RUN-ON SENTENCES

A ***run-on sentence*** is two sentences that are joined together incorrectly. Here are two examples:

> *Oil has many uses it can cause serious problems too.*

> *Oil has many uses, it can cause serious problems too.*

Look more closely at these examples. Each one is made up of two separate sentences.

> *Oil has many uses . . . it can cause serious problems too.*

You must use something to show that these are two separate sentences. You cannot use a comma all by itself. There are two ways to correct this run-on.

1. You can separate the two sentences completely:

   > *Oil has many uses. **It** can cause serious problems too.*

2. You can keep the sentences joined. To do this, you need to add a word like ***and*** or ***but*** along with a comma:

   > *Oil has many uses, **but** it can cause serious problems too.*

PRACTICE:

Correct these run-on sentences. Use method 1 for sentence 1. Use method 2 for sentence 2.

1. Petroleum is a popular fuel it is also used to make nylon and plastic.
2. Oil lies in pools under the ground, we can use pumps to bring it to the surface.

3. COMBINING SENTENCES

Combining sentences is a way of improving them. You can combine sentences to make them sound more interesting and to avoid repeating information:

UNCOMBINED: Amerigo Vespucci was well-known as a banker. He was well-known as a sailor.

COMBINED: Amerigo Vespucci was well-known as a banker and a sailor.

UNCOMBINED: The Spanish and Portuguese drew maps. The maps showed the new discoveries.

COMBINED: The Spanish and Portuguese drew maps to show the new discoveries.

When you combine sentences, watch out for two things:

1. Be sure to include all the information that is important.

2. Be careful not to make your new sentence too long or wordy.

   You may have to do these things:

   - Take out unnecessary words
   - Add words like ***and*** or ***but***

PRACTICE:

Combine each pair of sentences.

1. Amerigo Vespucci sailed with the Spanish in 1499. He sailed with the Portuguese in 1501.
2. Vespucci planned to cover his ships with lead. He wanted to cover them in order to protect them.

USAGE

TARGETS: ***Use the correct subject, object, and possessive forms of pronouns.***

Use correct subject-verb agreement with personal pronouns and compound subjects.

Recognize correct verb tense and correct form of irregular verbs.

Use the correct forms of adjectives and adverbs.

1. PRONOUN FORMS

A ***pronoun*** is a word like ***I***, or ***me***, or ***she***, or ***his***, or ***they***.

Pronouns have different forms. In order to choose the correct form, you need to look at how the pronoun is used in the sentence.

1. When the pronoun is the ***subject*** of a sentence, it has one of these forms:

   I like to walk dogs.

   You can earn money that way.

   He saved enough for a bicycle.

   She took care of four cats.

   It was not an easy job.

   We put up posters at the supermarket.

   They told about our pet-care service.

You might not be sure which form of the pronoun is correct when there is a ***compound subject*** (two or more subjects). Be careful to choose the subject form:

CORRECT: Nancy and ***she*** ran this business together.

INCORRECT: Nancy and ***her*** ran this business together.

HINT: When a pronoun is part of a compound subject, try saying the sentence with just one pronoun. "Nancy and her" might sound all right at first. But you can hear that it's wrong when you say it with just the pronoun: "Her ran this business."

PRACTICE:

Choose the correct form of the pronoun.

1. (They, Them) are my favorite kind of pet.
2. Carlos and (me, I) took turns brushing the dog.
3. (He, him) and Sara each made ten dollars.

2. When the pronoun is the object of a verb or a preposition, it has one of these forms:

Leroy gave ***me*** a new idea.

Did Ms. Anthony pay ***you*** right away?

Tell ***him*** how much the job will cost.

One of the dogs pushed ***her*** down.

Make ***it*** walk quietly on the leash.

The cats asked ***us*** for food.

Maria feeds ***them*** at five o'clock every day.

Again, watch out for compounds. Be careful to use the object form:

CORRECT: Mr. Gaines paid Fred and ***me***.

INCORRECT: Mr. Gaines paid Fred and ***I***.

If you are not sure which form is correct, try using the pronoun alone. "Mr. Gaines paid me" sounds all right. You can hear that "Mr. Gaines paid I" is wrong.

PRACTICE:

Choose the correct form of the pronoun.

4. The cat scratched both (he, him) and (she, her).
5. This job sounds just right for you and (me, I).

3. When the pronoun is used to show possession or ownership, it has one of these forms.

    My favorite job is helping in the yard.

    These gardening tools are ***mine***.

    Your bank account must be full of money now.

    Is this five-dollar bill ***yours***?

    His best customer is the man with the apple orchard.

    The house on High Street is ***his***.

    Her assistant waters the flowers first.

    Which rake is ***hers***?

    Its handle is cracked.

    Our job is almost done.

    That new shovel is ***ours***.

    Their price is too high.

    How much money is ***theirs***?

Here are two tricky things to watch out for:

- ***Hers, yours, ours, its,*** and ***theirs*** are NOT written with an apostrophe. (Other words are written with an apostrophe to show possession—*Jill's, anyone's*.)
- ***It's*** (with an apostrophe) stands for ***it is***.

PRACTICE:

Choose the correct form of the pronoun.

6. Two of these plants are (yours, your's).
7. The tree was beautiful when (its, it's) leaves turned red.
8. The picture of the wildflower garden was (hers, her's).

2. SUBJECT-VERB AGREEMENT

The form of a verb depends on two things:

- Whether the ***subject*** of the sentence is ***singular*** or ***plural***.
- Whether the verb shows an action in the present (***present tense***) or the past (***past tense***).

1. The present tense of a verb ends in ***-s*** or ***-es*** when the subject is a ***singular noun*** or one of these pronouns: ***he, she, it.***

   Nancy Lopez ***starts*** playing golf in the early morning.

   She ***finishes*** around dinner time.

NOTICE: The verbs ***have*** and ***do*** have special forms in the present tense:

   Ms. Lopez ***has*** a long, tiring day.

   She ***does*** more than play golf.

2. The present tense of the verb does NOT have an ***-s*** or an ***-es*** ending added to it when the subject is a ***plural noun*** or one of these pronouns: ***I, we, you, they.***

   Fans ***visit*** the golfing Hall of Fame.

   They ***watch*** her play on television.

3. A ***compound subject*** (two or more subjects) is like a plural subject. The present tense of the verb does not have ***-s*** or ***-es*** added to it.

   Diet and exercise ***help*** her stay fit.

   She and her children ***spend*** time together every day.

PRACTICE:

Choose the correct form of the verb.

1. Judge Sosa (live, lives) in New Mexico.
2. He (have, has) seven children.
3. The Judge and his wife also (have, has) many grandchildren.
4. The judges (discuss, discusses) cases from all over the state.
5. Mr. and Mrs. Sosa (do, does) all they can to help other Mexican-Americans.

3. The verb ***be*** is special. It has different forms in both the present tense and the past tense. Make sure you know which forms go with singular subjects and which forms go with plural subjects.

WHEN THE SUBJECT IS ***SINGULAR:***

Present Tense	Past Tense
I am	I was
You are	You were
He/she/it is	He/she/it was
The game is	The game was

WHEN THE SUBJECT IS ***PLURAL:***

Present Tense	Past Tense
We are	We were
You are	You were
They are	They were
The games are	The games were

PRACTICE:

1. Willie Velasquez (was, were) from Texas.
2. The story of his life (is, are) interesting.
3. Willie's grandfather (was, were) Mexican.
4. Willie and his grandparents (was, were) neighbors.
5. San Antonio (is, are) the city they lived in.

3. VERB TENSES AND THE FORMS OF IRREGULAR VERBS

1. The form of a verb (called its ***tense***) shows the time when the action of the sentence takes place:

   Today ***is*** Monday. (present tense)

   Yesterday ***was*** Sunday. (past tense)

When you write about something that happened in the past, be sure to use the past tense of the verb. Don't write sentences where the tense is wrong for the meaning of the sentence:

WRONG: Yesterday is Sunday.

2. Most verbs add ***-d*** or ***-ed*** at the end to show past time:

Katherine Ortega ***worked*** as an accountant.

Her sister had ***managed*** the family restaurant.

Other verbs are ***irregular.*** They form their past tense in different ways:

The Ortega family ***took*** pride in what their children did.

Katherine had ***become*** head of the U.S. Mint.

The President had ***chosen*** her for this job.

People ***saw*** her name on their money.

If the verb is irregular, be careful to choose the correct form. On the following page is a list of irregular verbs. Study it carefully; then come back and do the Practice exercises below.

PRACTICE:

Choose the correct form of the verb.

1. When he (is, was) little, his grandfather (tell, told) him wonderful stories.
2. He and his brothers (grew, growed) up and (go, went) to the big city to live.
3. She has (want, wanted) to be a baseball player since the first time she (throw, threw) a ball.
4. As soon as she had (gave, given) her speech, everyone (began, begun) to applaud.
5. Everyone she (knew, known) has (thunk, thought) she would be a success.

IRREGULAR VERBS

PRESENT TENSE	PAST TENSE	
become	became	has become
begin	began	has begun
bet	bet	has bet
blow	blew	has blown
break	broke	has broken
bring	brought	has brought
burst	burst	has burst
buy	bought	has bought
catch	caught	has caught
choose	chose	has chosen
come	came	has come
cut	cut	has cut
dive	dived, dove	has dived
do	did	has done
eat	ate	has eaten
fly	flew	has flown
forget	forgot	has forgot, forgotten
give	gave	has given
go	went	has gone
grow	grew	has grown
hang	hung	has hung
have	had	has had
hit	hit	has hit
hurt	hurt	has hurt
know	knew	has known
let	let	has let
mean	meant	has meant
ride	rode	has ridden
ring	rang	has rung
rise	rose	has risen
run	ran	has run
see	saw	has seen
shine	shone	has shone
sing	sang	has sung
spring	sprang, sprung	has sprung
stink	stank	has stunk
strike	struck	has struck
swim	swam	has swum
take	took	has taken
tell	told	has told
think	thought	has thought
throw	threw	has thrown
write	wrote	has written

4. FORMS OF ADJECTIVES AND ADVERBS

Adjectives describe or tell about nouns or pronouns:

> His face was ***sad***, with ***big*** eyes and a ***droopy red*** mouth.

Adverbs describe or tell about verbs, adjectives, or other adverbs. They often answer the question "How?"

> The clown shuffled ***sadly*** onto the stage. His eyes were ***really*** big, and he moved ***very*** slowly.

Most adverbs end in ***-ly***. In fact, many adverbs are formed by adding ***-ly*** to an adjective:

> tight***ly*** clever***ly*** soft***ly*** safe***ly***

1. A common mistake is to use an adjective in place of an adverb. Here are some examples:

CORRECT: Her costume is ***really*** colorful.

INCORRECT: Her costume is ***real*** colorful.

CORRECT: I can't see the stage too ***well***.

INCORRECT: I can't see the stage too ***good***.

CORRECT: He sings that song ***terribly***.

INCORRECT: He sings that song ***terrible***.

PRACTICE:

Choose the correct word.

1. First, hold (tight, tightly) to this pole.
2. Then step (careful, carefully) onto the tightrope.
3. Say each line (clear, clearly) when you tell a joke.
4. The audience should be able to hear you (good, well).
5. Your act is (real, really) professional now.

2. Both adjectives and adverbs can be used to compare people or things.

   - Use ***-er*** or ***more*** when you compare two people or things:

     *Your clown act will be **funnier** if you walk on stilts.*

     *It will also be **more interesting.***

   However, you will not walk ***more quickly*** than you did before.

HINT: If you add ***-er***, do not use ***more***.

   - Use ***-est*** or ***most*** when you compare more than two people or things.

     *Stilts will make you the **tallest** person in the circus.*

     *They might even make your act the **most enjoyable** one of all.*

     *You can fasten your stilts the **most securely** of all with Velcro.*

HINT: If you add ***-est***, do not use ***most***.

   - Most one-syllable words add ***-er*** and ***-est***. Most words with two or more syllables use ***more*** and ***most.***

     tall, taller, tallest

     helpful, more helpful, most helpful

     powerful, more powerful, most powerful

   But words of two syllables that end in ***-y*** usually take ***-er*** and ***-est***.

     funny, funnier, funniest

PRACTICE:

Choose the correct form.

1. Wanda juggles (more easily, more easier) now that she has practiced.
2. Ivan is the (silliest, most silliest) clown of all.
3. You need to take yourself (more serious, more seriously) if you want to succeed.
4. Ronald's pants are (baggier, more baggier) than Donald's.
5. Olga handles the spinning plates (most gentle, most gently) of all.

***TARGET:* Use the fundamentals of spelling.**

One letter is missing from each of the words in the list below.

1. Complete the words you know.
2. Put a question mark beside the words you don't know.
3. Use a dictionary to check your work and to help you complete the words you didn't know.
4. The words you marked with a question and the words you got wrong are your **problem words.**

Learn these words by:

- writing them in list form
- using each one in a sentence
- printing the word and the sentence on a flash card
- applying the "3S" technique:

  Say the word, pronouncing each sound

  Spell the word

  Say the word again

---

abo__t
addr__ss
adv__se
aga__n
a__l right
alon__
alre__dy
altho__gh
alway__
am__ng

Apr__l
arithm__tic
a__nt
__while
ba__loon
b__cause
be__n
b__fore
b__rthday
blu__

boug__t
bu__lt
bus__ness
bus__
childr__n
choc__late
choo__e
Chris__mas
clos__
col__r

com__
c__ming
cou__h
cou__d
could__'t
co__ntry
cous__n
cu__board
da__ly
decorat__

des__ert
didn__t
doct__r
do__s
e__rly
E__ster
e__sy
eno__gh
ev__ry
ever__body

fav__rite
Feb__uary
f__erce
firs__
fo__tball
fo__ty
fo__rth
Fr__day
fri__nd
fue__

---

get__ing
go__s
grad__
g__ard
g__ess
ha__f
Hal__oween
handkerchi__f
hav__n't
hav__ng

he__r
h__ard
heig__t
hel__o
__ere
hospit__l
__our
hous__
inste__d
k__ew

k__ow
la__d
lat__er
les__ons
let__er
lit__le
lo__se
lov__ng
mak__ng
m__ny

---

mayb__
minut__
mor__ing
mo__her
nam__
ne__ther
nic__
non__
o'clo__k
o__f

of__en
onc__
outs__de
p__rty
peac__
pe__ple
pi__ce
play__d
__lays
ple__se

pois__n
pract__ce
pr__tty
princip__l
q__arter
qu__t
quit__
rais__
r__ad
re__dy

rec__ive
rece__ved
rem__mber
rig__t
r__ugh
rout__
sa__d
Santa Cla__s
Sat__rday
s__ys
s__hool
sc__oolhouse
sev__ral
sho__s
s__nce
ski__ng
__kis
som__
somet__ing
som__time
so__n
stor__
stra__ght
stud__ing
sug__r
sum__er
Sund__y
sup__ose
sur__
sur__ly

- - - - - - - - - - - - - - - - - - - -

s__rprise
sur__ounded
swim__ing
te__cher
te__r
ter__ible
Thanksg__ving
the__
ther__
th__y
thou__h
thoug__t
thro__gh
tir__d
togeth__r
tomor__ow
ton__ght
tra__n
trav__ling
tro__ble
tr__ly
Tu__sday
tw__
unt__l
us__d
v__cation
ver__
we__r
we__ther
we__gh

- - - - - - - - - - - - - - - - - - - -

wer__
we'r__
w__en
w__ere
w__ich
whit__
whol__
wom__n
wou__d
writ__
writ__ng
__rote
y__u
yo__r
you'__e

CAPITALIZATION

TARGET: Use the appropriate capitalization.

1. Capitalize the first word in a sentence.

   Last spring our class went to Austin.

   This rule is tricky only when you write more than one sentence. You might not notice the missing capital:

   Our class goes on many field trips. last spring we took a special trip.

HINT: When you see a period at the end of a sentence, look for a capital letter to follow.

2. Capitalize the pronoun ***I*** wherever it appears.

   Maria and **I** sat together on the school bus.

   Not every language capitalizes this pronoun. French and Spanish, for example, do not. If you use another language, remember to capitalize this pronoun when you write English.

3. Capitalize a title used before a person's name.

   First we met with **R**epresentative Darcy. Then we talked to **S**enator Roybal.

   Here are some other titles. Fill in the blanks with names you know.

   President ______ **G**overnor ______

   General ______ **C**olonel ______

   Officer ______ **D**octor ______

4. Capitalize each important word in the title of a written work.

   Before our trip we read the book **T**exas **L**awmakers.

5. Capitalize the first word in a direct quotation.

   The senator said, "**W**e are going to vote now."

6. Capitalize proper nouns.

   We learned how laws were made in **T**exas when we visited the **S**tate **L**egislature in **A**pril.

Here are some other kinds of proper nouns. Write an example of your own for each one.

a street name	**S**antiago **R**oad	____________
a language	**S**panish	____________
a building	the **A**lamo	____________
a country	**V**ietnam	____________
animal breed	**H**ereford	____________
geographical	**R**io **G**rande	____________
feature	**F**alcon **L**ake	____________
a business	**H**ouston **P**ower	____________
	& **L**ight **C**ompany	____________
a school	**R**ice **L**earning	____________
	Center	____________
a state	**A**labama	____________
a city	**B**rownsville	____________

Can you think of any other categories to add to this list?

There are two other rules you will need to know for the TAAS test. These rules are used when you write letters.

7. Capitalize the first word in a letter opening.
8. Capitalize the first word in the closing of a letter.

> **D**ear Senator Luray:
>
> Thank you for showing us how laws are made in Texas. Our visit to the Texas State Legislature was the best field trip we had this year.
>
> **Y**ours truly,
>
> *Grade 5*

PRACTICE:

Which words in the following sentences should be capitalized?

1. Have you ever been to corpus christi?
2. It is the largest coastal city in texas.
3. You can visit padre island too.
4. Treasure from spanish ships has been found there.
5. Our guide asked, "who wants to see where they found the treasure?"
6. Of course i wanted to see the place.
7. You have to be lucky to find treasure. you also have to know what you are looking for.
8. The book buried treasure explains how to use old maps to find sunken ships.
9. Which words in this letter should be capitalized?

> dear officer Bradner,
>
> Thank you for visiting our class last week. We learned how to be safe and sane bike riders from your talk.
>
> yours truly,
>
> *Grade 5*

PUNCTUATION

TARGET: Use the fundamentals of punctuation.

1. END PUNCTUATION (PERIOD, QUESTION MARK, EXCLAMATION POINT)

End Punctuation is used to indicate that something is finished.

1. Use a ***period*** (**.**) at the end of a statement or a command.

   The next stop on our tour was Kingsville, Texas**.**

   Take Exit 17 to Route 512**.**

2. Use a period at the end of an abbreviation.

St**.** _______	Mr**.** _______
Dr**.** _______	Ave**.** _______
Lt**.** _______	Rev**.** _______

   What does each abbreviation mean?

3. Use a ***question mark*** at the end of a question.

   Can you get to the King Ranch from here**?**

4. Use an ***exclamation*** at the end of a sentence that shows strong feeling.

   What a huge state Texas is**!**

2. COMMAS

Commas are used to separate.

1. Use a ***comma*** between words in a series of three or more things.

    The state flag of Texas is red, white, and blue with a white star in the center.

2. Use a comma before a direct quotation.

    The state trooper said, "Get off at the next exit and turn left."

3. Use a comma between the day and year in a date.

    June 13, 1991

    July 4, 1776

4. Use a comma between city and state.

    Galveston, Texas

The last two comma rules are used only when you write a letter.

5. Use a comma after the opening of a friendly letter.
6. Use a comma after the closing of a letter.

    Dear Martha,

    Thanks for your invitation. We'll see you in August at your place in Houston. We can hardly wait!

    Love,

    Kay & Chuck

3. APOSTROPHES

1. Use an ***apostrophe*** in possessives.

   We stopped by the river's edge.

   Sam took off the dogs' collars and let them run.

2. Use an apostrophe in contractions.

didn't _______	weren't _______	_______
can't _______	won't _______	_______
isn't _______	aren't _______	_______

What do these contractions mean? Add some more to the list above.

PRACTICE:

Add punctuation where it is needed.

1. Have you ever been to the Rio Grande Valley
2. Brownsville Texas was our starting point.
3. We left on July 27 1991.
4. What a hot place Texas is in the summer
5. Ms. Santario at the Rio Grande Valley Information Bureau told us what to see and do.
6. She said "You be sure to try our grapefruit."
7. We stopped in Weslaco McAllen and Mission and bought red grapefruit.
8. Later we went to the rivers edge and skipped stones.
9. Sam and Verna didnt want to leave the valley.
10. They liked the people and the places they saw.

Put the missing commas in this letter:

11.

Amarillo Texas

August 10 1991

Dear Verne

Aren't you ever coming back? I know you like the valley, but school is starting next week.

Love

Mom

SENTENCE CONSTRUCTION

1. Incomplete Sentences (Sentence Fragments)

1. correct sentence
2. fragment: When . . . captivity

2. Run-on Sentences

1. Petroleum is a popular fuel. It is also used to make nylon and plastic.
2. Oil lies in pools under the ground, but we can use pumps to bring it to the surface.

3. Combining Sentences

1. Amerigo Vespucci sailed with the Spanish in 1499 and with the Portuguese in 1501.
2. Vespucci planned to cover his ships with lead in order to protect them.

USAGE

1. Pronoun Forms

1. They
2. I
3. He
4. him, her
5. me
6. yours
7. its
8. hers

2. Subject-Verb Agreement

1. lives
2. has
3. have
4. discuss
5. do
6. was
7. is
8. was
9. were
10. is

3. Verb Tenses and the Forms of Irregular Verbs

1. was, told
2. grew, went
3. wanted, threw
4. given, began.
5. knew, thought

4. Forms of Adjectives and Adverbs

1. heavily
2. carefully
3. clearly
4. well
5. really
6. more easily
7. silliest
8. more seriously
9. baggier
10. most gently

CAPITALIZATION

1. Have you ever been to Corpus Christi?
2. It is the largest coastal city in Texas.
3. You can visit Padre Island too.
4. Treasure from Spanish ships has been found there.
5. Our guide asked, "Who wants to see where they found the treasure?"
6. Of course I wanted to see the place.
7. You have to be lucky to find treasure. You also have to know what you are looking for.
8. The book Buried Treasure explains how to use old maps to find sunken ships.
9. Dear Officer Bradner,

   Thank you for visiting our class last week. We learned how to be safe and sane bike riders from your talk.

   Yours truly,
   Grade 5

PUNCTUATION

1. Have you ever been to the Rio Grande Valley**?**
2. Brownsville**,** Texas**,** was the starting point of our trip.
3. We left on July 27**,** 1991.
4. What a hot place Texas is in the summer**!**
5. OK as is
6. She said**,** "You be sure to try our grapefruit**.**"
7. We stopped in Weslaco**,** McAllen**,** and Mission and bought red grapefruit. *(Some people don't use the second comma.)*
8. Later we went to the river**'**s edge and threw stones as far as we could.
9. Sam and Verna didn**'**t want to leave the valley.
10. They liked the people and the places they had seen**.**
11. Amarillo**,** Texas
    August 10**,** 1997

    Dear Verne**,**

    Aren't you ever coming back? I know you like the valley, but school is starting next week.

    Love**,**
    Mom